DISCIPLINE

r Today's Children and Youth

ge V. Sheviakov and Fritz Redl

NEW REVISION
BY
SYBIL K. RICHARDSON

OCIATION FOR SUPERVISION AND CURRICULUM DEVELOPMENT, NEA

Introducing the Authors . . .

Coming to America from Russia, GEORGE V. SHEVIAKOV attended the universities of Washington and California. At the University of California Institute of Child Welfare, he was engaged in a research study of 125 babies and their families during a period of seven years. Later he saw these children when they were adolescents.

The recipient of a fellowship awarded by the General Education Board, Rockefeller Foundation, Mr. Sheviakov devoted two years to the Study of Adolescents, conducted by the Progressive Education Association in New York City. For three years he was a member of the evaluation staff of the Eight Year Study and for two years was guidance counselor in the University of Chicago Laboratory Schools. He has also been associated with the Study of the Southern Association of Secondary Schools and Colleges. When World War II broke out, Mr. Sheviakov became assistant superintendent of schools in Vanport, Oregon, a housing development for Kaiser shipyard workers. Since 1946 he has been lecturer in psychology at San Francisco State College. He has worked extensively as a consultant with teachers and administrators in California on their day-by-day problems.

FRITZ REDL came to this country from Austria in 1936 to do research for the Rockefeller Foundation, along with Mr. Sheviakov, in the field of adolescence. Educated at the University of Vienna, he brought with him years of extensive training and experience in education and psychoanalysis. He taught in the public schools of Vienna for ten years and lectured widely in Europe on topics relating to education, child psychiatry, and guidance. In the United States, he has engaged in research projects and has been on the staff of the universities of Michigan and Chicago, Wayne University, and numerous summer workshops. He has lectured widely and is author of many publications, both in English and German. Since 1941 he has been professor of social work at Wayne University, Detroit. He developed an agency for clinical group work and group therapy with children (the Detroit Group Project and the Detroit Group Project Summer Camp) and a treatment home (Pioneer House). He is now Chief of the Child Research Branch at The Clinical Center of the National Institute of Health, Bethesda, Maryland.

SYBIL K. RICHARDSON studied psychology and education at Mills College, California, and at the University of California at Los Angeles. As a clinical psychologist in the California State Child Guidance Clinic and on the staff of the Los Angeles County Superintendent of Schools, she has long been interested in helping teachers to understand deviant and disturbed children. This interest has extended to general in-service education through work with teachers in their own schools and at Claremont College, Stanford University, the University of California at Los Angeles, and the University of Southern California. Mrs. Richardson writes for education periodicals on both guidance and curriculum topics. She is co-author of "Childhood Problems and the Teacher" and has contributed to "Educating the Children of Los Angeles County," a course of study, and teachers guide.

DISCIPLINE

For Today's Children and Youth

George V. Sheviakov and Fritz Redl

NEW REVISION
BY
SYBIL K. RICHARDSON

ASSOCIATION FOR SUPERVISION AND CURRICULUM DEVELOPMENT
A department of the National Education Association
1201 Sixteenth Street, N. W., Washington 6, D. C.

Contents

Foreword

DISCIPLINE FOR TODAY'S CHILDREN AND YOUTH, first issued in 1944, has had more than 30 reprintings. Clearly, teachers and parents, eager to gain new insight into the theory and practice of democratic discipline, have found help in this booklet. The Association for Supervision and Curriculum Development, NEA, is glad indeed to publish this new revision of such sound and useful material.

Schools in the next decade must foster in children and young people the intellectual and moral discipline needed for preserving and strengthening our democratic way of life. The Association hopes this booklet will help teachers and parents in these critical years.

We are grateful to Fritz Redl and George V. Sheviakov for writing the original pamphlet and for their glad consent to its revision. Their psychological and psychoanalytic training and their experience in working with children and young people have enabled them to make practical and vivid application of psychological theory to problems which arise as teachers and children work together in the classroom. Part I was originally written by George V. Sheviakov, while Part II was by Fritz Redl. In this revision there has been some merging of these two parts, though to a large extent their original authorship still holds.

Sybil K. Richardson deserves high praise for her excellent revision of this booklet. Her experience in helping teachers to understand the implications of child growth and development for the school program enable her to explain effectively the relationship which should exist between practice and sound theory.

John I. Goodlad, Chairman, ASCD Publications Committee, read and made critical suggestions on the revised manuscript. Robert R. Leeper, Associate Secretary and Editor, ASCD, and Lorraine Alleman, Editorial Assistant, NEA Publications Division, edited the manuscript and guided it through publication. The title page is the work of de Graffenried W. List, Artist, NEA Publications Division.

ROBERT S. GILCHRIST, *President, ASCD*
For the Executive Committee

August 1956

PART I

Let's Look at Discipline

Problems of discipline and self-control assume a new significance and realism in today's world. In a complex civilization, the individual often has to subjugate his personal inclinations, whims, comforts, even some of his liberties to bigger goals than personal ones. In the uncertainty of a "divided world" where peaceful coexistence of conflicting philosophies of life may at any time be terminated by armed conflict, the individual must be ready to renounce for the good of the group even his wish to survive. If the democratic philosophy is to flourish, our ways of living and believing, the ideals of generations must be preserved. For this we need children and young people who cherish these ideals above all and who, therefore, are ready to endure privation and to exercise the utmost self-control.

How can we help children and youth develop the intellectual and moral discipline essential to a free people? If we adults are not to make serious errors we too have to exercise discipline of mind. We must think through carefully and clearly what we mean by discipline, what kind of discipline we want, and by what methods we can best achieve it.

In the face of uncertainty many persons tend to regress to simple and primitive ways of dealing with difficulties. In times of strain and anxiety there are demands for speeded-up action. Patient educational procedures, the making of complex judgments, are likely to be neglected. Instead, people begin to look for a less thought-requiring procedure. Some begin to look for a scale in which there is a prescribed form of punishment for every specific misdemeanor. Others advocate such coercive techniques as return to "woodshed" whippings, military marching in schools, more drill in the 3 R's, or fining parents of children who get into trouble. These solutions are appealing because they seem simple and definite. They are ineffective in the long run, however, because they do not teach children right ways of behaving when coercion is removed. It is because of such confusions that we must examine very carefully the concept of "discipline" and our own practices with children and youth.

Thinking Straight About Discipline

The word discipline has different meanings. Webster's Dictionary gives the following four as the most common of eight meanings listed.

The treatment suited to a disciple or learner; education; development of the faculties by instructing and exercise.

Training to act in accordance with established rules; accustoming to systematic and regular action; drill.

Subjection to rule; submissiveness to order and control; control; habit of obedience.

Correction; chastisement inflicted by way of correction and training; hence training through suffering.

We note here that the first two definitions are relatively broad and that they do not necessarily imply the imposition of a will of one person upon another; neither do they prescribe a specific method. "Treatment," "education," "development," "training," "accustoming" may or may not be methods compatible with self-respect, integrity and relative freedom of the person in training. The third and fourth definitions, however, prescribe subjugation to the will of another and deny freedom of the person by the terms "habit of obedience," and "chastisement." The fourth even prescribes specifically the method of training "through suffering." The several meanings given the word reflect and increase people's confusion in thinking about discipline.

While a variety of meanings for the word discipline is given in the dictionary, teachers seem to use it in their talks at the luncheon table or in staff meetings in three different ways:

Meaning No. 1. In this sense we mean by "discipline" the *degree* of order we have established in a group. Thus we say: "Miss X doesn't seem to have much discipline in her seventh grade." Or, "Mr. Y doesn't seem to me to know so much about his field, but he sure has a lot of discipline in his classroom. I must say that for him." In both cases we usually use the verb "to have" in conjunction with discipline. *By* *the "discipline we have" we usually refer to the degree of organization* we have achieved in a group. The question of just *how* we have obtained this organized functioning of a group is left open.

Meaning No. 2. In this sense we mean by "discipline" not the order we have, but *the trick by which we have established order.* For instance, "Say, Miss Jones, what discipline do you use in your grade?" or "She has a good homeroom, but I don't quite like the discipline she uses." In both cases we usually find the word "use" in conjunction with the word discipline. By the *"discipline we use"* we mean: *anything we do to establish, maintain, or repair order in our groups.*

It is obvious how misleading such double use of the word discipline can be. No wonder we get confused, if at times we use the same word to point to the *order we want to establish* and at other times to point to the *technique by which* we establish that order. This is why there is so much controversy among teachers over something which is a problem of simple semantics.

Meaning No. 3. In this sense people often use the word—the verb especially—as a euphemism for *punishment.* "I am sorry there wasn't anything I could do with him any more. I simply had to discipline him." Or, "Don't you think that children should be disciplined at times?" In these cases we do *not* talk about order, but about a special way of enforcing it. And among the dozens of ways of encouraging the growth of order, we mean simply one, as though it were the only one, namely, punishment.

This is, of course, a most fallacious use of the term. When it happens along with other uses of the term in the same discussion, we may easily see what confusions arise:

Mr. A: I don't agree with the way you disciplined Johnny the other day. I think this is only going to make him more stubborn than he already is.

Mr. B: What! Don't you believe in discipline?

The solution of such a misunderstanding is simple if we perceive the dual meanings; there is no such alternative as Mr. B suggests. Belief in discipline as order or organization does not mean belief that only one method, that of punishment, is the right way to get it, in spite of the identity of terms.

Thinking straight about discipline requires that we *know* just which way we or other speakers use the term, or we shall never get beyond a Babelic confusion in our discussions. For use in this bulletin we shall eliminate meaning No. 3: When we mean punishment, we shall say punishment instead of hiding it under terminological disguises.

We shall, however, have to talk about both of the other meanings at different places. But we shall always add specific enough statements to make it clear just what we are talking about at the time, whether discipline as a certain type of order, or as the technique we use to establish, maintain, repair it. Major misunderstandings can be easily avoided as long as we make clear which of these two meanings we intend.

Discipline must have a goal. The use of the word discipline as order leaves open to our choice which method of attaining discipline we will adopt. To clarify our thinking we must recognize first that discipline is always connected with a goal or purpose. The attainment of a goal which is too big to be reached immediately by the individual involves discipline. The saving of pennies for a pocket knife, and the patient building of a toy airplane are examples of a child's control of his impulses for a broader goal and satisfaction than can be attained through following an immediate impulse, by stealing a knife or buying a ready-made airplane. Thus discipline may be thought of as organization of one's impulses for the attainment of a goal.

Group discipline demands control of impulses of the individuals composing a group for the attainment of a goal which all have accepted. The latter is always a goal which cannot be achieved singly by any one person. Waiting for the family's dinner hour, singing with others, and putting on a play are simple situations in which discipline is dictated by the goal to be achieved by a group.

At different ages people are ready for different goals. The more mature and fully developed the person is, the longer he is capable of waiting; and the more complex and socialized will be the source of his eventual satisfaction. Thus putting money aside for old age demands more intricate organization than saving money for a pocket knife, and readiness to endure hardships for an ideal or principle is on a broader social level than participating in a play. This leads us to the realization that the goals for which discipline is required vary in complexity and that these goals also change with age.

Different goals are pursued differently. Behavior which is appropriate for one goal may not be suitable when the goal or purpose of discipline changes. We may illustrate this by the following example: When a troop of Boy Scouts practices marching, the goal for the group is to act symmetrically, in unison, and discipline or order shows itself through the symmetry achieved. When, however, the same group climbs a mountain, the goal is not symmetry of action but the scaling of the mountain. This group can walk loosely. Individual members may chase a butterfly, or examine rocks and plants. As long as they do not get lost, and thus interfere with the group goal, they are still well disciplined for the goal in mind.

Running through the hall on a Saturday afternoon to get to a Scout meeting on time is one kind of appropriate behavior to maintain discipline. Running through the same hall during recess on a school day indicates poor discipline because it interferes with the group goal of the moment—that everyone shall get to his class safely and efficiently.

Too often in our discussions of discipline we concentrate on specific acts and talk of these behaviors as being indicative of good or poor discipline. We forget that these acts must be evaluated in terms of the individual or group goal to be achieved at a particular time. Indeed, in every discussion of discipline we should ask: "Discipline for what?" For the truly well-disciplined person does not behave in a rigid manner regardless of the circumstances around him. He is able intelligently to select from his entire repertory of behavior the actions which are most appropriate for his personal or group goal.

What Kind of Discipline Do We Want?

We see now that this question can be answered only if we decide on the goal we have in view. Most persons would agree readily that in our times the primary goal of all education, at home as well as in school, is the fullest realization of every person's potential. It is only through the development of individual capacities that the truly American and democratic way of living can be preserved and extended.

In spite of this general agreement, thoughtful persons have observed that we have not analyzed sufficiently what it is that we love and cherish in our country. We must analyze consciously and rationally the many specific differences between our democratic philosophy and an autocratic or totalitarian way of life. The more clearly we understand this the better job we will do with children and youth.

To understand better the difference between the democratic and the autocratic philosophies, it is helpful to trace the development of individuals reared under favorable circumstances in a civilized community. If we do this, we observe that there are certain developmental steps through which human beings progress in the process of civilized maturation. These steps are not too sharply defined, for some of the attitudes of adults begin to be formed even in early childhood. Nevertheless, we can view human development as a series of steps from self-centeredness to a gradual broadening and deepening of capacity to feel for others. This is the essence of our emotional growth and one of the major aspects of spiritual growth. Outlining these developmental periods roughly, one may speak of the following steps:

1. Period of self-centeredness and self-love characteristic of infancy.

2. Gradual development of love for mother, first as comforter and source of pleasure, and later as an object of affection for whom small sacrifices are made by the child. This affection gradually spreads out to include the father and other persons in the child's immediate environment. This development is characteristic of childhood, providing it is a happy one.

3. Gradually the child reaches the club or gang stage during which he forms strong attachments and at times great loyalties to a group most like himself—typically other children of the same sex. Ordinarily, this takes place in the intermediate grades.

4. During the next stage—adolescence—most children broaden still further and develop strong friendly feelings to their contemporaries of the opposite sex, as well as to groups of young people of both sexes. The group becomes a "clique" or a "set" and is now rather similar to adult friendship groupings. Nevertheless, romantic love during this period is rather self-centered and although the adolescent's society is much broader than it was during the "gang" stage, social problems which concern the adult do not yet have much meaning for the younger person.

5. A still further social development takes place gradually in the young adult who develops a capacity for intense attachments to a mate, his children, his church, club, or professional group. Interest in the affairs and welfare of his community, his state, and his country are usually developed sooner or later during this phase. As unselfish as the young adult may be in these affections, the element of "my" family, "my" home state, is still quite important.

6. The last stage of development goes far beyond that described above. Here the person extends his loyalties completely beyond himself and his immediate associates. He becomes devoted to such ideals and concepts as justice, liberty, tolerance, sympathy for the downtrodden and other broad human values. In a highly mature and socialized person, humanity and human values are placed above personal gain, comfort and personal loyalties. A principle or an ideal becomes even more important than one's group, one's friend, one's family.

Authoritarian social philosophy stops short of the last developmental aim or ideal described. In some autocratic societies, education does not aim at developing ideals of equality but substitutes the concept of a master race or privileged class. Youths in such societies

are trained systematically to treat with indignity those not like themselves, racially or ideologically. In such societies the leaders are generally drawn only from certain privileged groups. Youth is trained in
loyalty and obedience to strong and forceful leaders.

In other authoritarian societies the interests of the individual are
subordinated to those of the state. The individual's talents, desires and
aspirations are considered less important than the needs and demands
of the body politic. In such societies the development of individuality
is encouraged or tolerated only when it is to the advantage of the
larger group.

A democracy is distinguished from both kinds of authoritarian societies by its solicitude for every individual. Differences are not only
accepted, but are valued for the contribution which they can make
to the welfare and progress of all. In a democracy there is no real
conflict between the value placed upon the individual and the ideals
of group life. Only as each individual's potential is realized can the
optimum welfare for all be approached. Only in the good state which
shows concern for every citizen can each person develop his full
capacities. The democratic society is unique in its recognition of the
interdependence of the individual and the group.

Returning to our original problem we may say that in authoritarian
societies education, social philosophy and goals, and preparation for
these goals are very different than in ours. Our discipline, therefore,
has to be different from theirs. Our goals or ideals are infinitely more
advanced, and in dealing with the youth of our time we must be
scrupulously careful not to tinge our ideals and methods with this
authoritarian philosophy. We do not want to train our youth to follow
leaders slavishly. We want them to follow principles in their clearest
form and in line with the ideals of those men and women who have
helped to evolve our way of life and our way of feeling about life and
human beings.

In the light of what has been said above, then, what kind of discipline do we want?

1. We want discipline which recognizes the *inherent dignity and rights*
of every human being, rather than discipline attained through humiliation
of the undisciplined.

2. We want discipline based on *devotion to humanitarian principles and
ideals.* In a democratic society, loyalty to the principles of freedom, justice
and equality for all rather than discipline based on a narrower, more
egotistic affiliation of "*my* group" is essential.

3. We want *self-direction, self-discipline,* rather than discipline based
upon unquestioning obedience to a leader.

4. We want discipline based on *understanding* of the goal in view rather than discipline based on taking someone else's word for specific appropriate behaviors.

Growth Toward Self-Guidance

So far we have attempted to clarify the meaning of the word "discipline" and to define the kind of discipline that we want. We want youth highly disciplined democratically, that is, young people who behave effectively toward the attainment of a democratic way of life as a main goal. A difficult problem still remains—what are the best methods of attaining this kind of highly disciplined American youth? Is it necessary, for instance, to use temporarily essentially undemocratic methods with immature youth, or is there a way for us to use methods which are consistent with our ideals?

In discussing methods we may be helped if we trace some of the changes which evolve as a society grows closer to its democratic ideals. We have already traced the development of the individual to see more clearly the steps through which the democratic personality is fostered. As has been mentioned, no clear-cut lines mark these developmental steps. Some of the traits characteristic of an early stage may continue side by side with some of the more advanced achievements of our personality. All adults may be said to be also children in those respects.

Just as individuals, at any stage of maturation, retain some of the characteristics of preceding stages, and just as the same person will have prominent in his personality different and often conflicting characteristics, so in our society and in our social thinking we are spotty and uneven. Most of us tend to practice side by side the more primitive and autocratic as well as the more democratic and advanced methods of dealing with our fellow men. We must remember this as we think the problem through to the best of our ability and as far as our own development permits us. We must not forget that the stage of our own social development has a great deal to do with our beliefs about discipline. Therefore, in re-examining these beliefs let us also review the progress which our society has made.

All Americans will agree that they believe in democracy. They will vary greatly, however, in the extent to which they apply principles of democracy in their daily living with their families, with their co-workers, their superiors, and with those in their charge. We should like to invite every reader to ask himself how often he says, "Yes, I believe in democracy, but . . . we must be realistic." Realism is of greatest importance, but this phrase is frequently used to cover an unwillingness to apply in life what the person professes to believe.

Even so, as falteringly as we go ahead, certain changes are clearly visible in democracy's methods of educating civilized citizens. It is undeniable that, as our culture develops, the methods and ways of dealing with human beings who do not comply with our standards are changing. This change is consistently in one direction, of avoiding subjecting persons to indignities. Acceptance of belief in the inherent dignity of every human being is penetrating deeper and deeper into the thinking and feeling of the masses of our population. From simple and primitive punitive concepts we have come quite generally to concepts of correction and prevention. Torture, physical punishment, public humiliation of the lawbreaker, which naturally flare up under the authoritarian philosophy, are almost without exception things of the past in our country. Jails, for instance, are concerned not with various ways of punishing the offender, but with techniques of guidance and rehabilitation to bring the offender back into society.

Instead of the adage, "Spare the rod and spoil the child," parents are taught that their own self-discipline, setting an example, showing affection toward their children, and taking time out to play and talk and work together will produce the best results—the most civilized children. Some of the largest and most successful industries, instead of the old methods of fining and firing, have devised systems of personal counseling, with employees sharing in the welfare of the organization through group insurances, or other benefits.

When we stop to think, we realize how far we have progressed in a relatively short time. Other practices were current even within our own lifetime. But we have made rapid progress and have made progress in an age in which a good portion of the world population has regressed to primitive, incredibly barbaric points of view, attitudes, and practices. We may be truly proud of the job we have done as a nation. Let us cherish this attainment as we attempt to share it with those who, because of ignorance and immaturity, may have been tempted by an anti- or non-democratic philosophy.

Democratic Principles Guide Our Practices

The principles of democratic living guide our practices as we help children grow toward self-discipline and self-direction. We must not only know what we believe, but learn to live every day according to those beliefs. For principles have meaning only as they are practiced in daily living. Maxims and precepts, however inspired, influence our behavior only when they are exemplified in countless incidents throughout our lives. The teacher who is skillful in educating for discipline, continuously analyzes and relates classroom practices to the democratic principles we seek to instill in all children and youth.

Principle I.

Faith in the worth and dignity of every human being is the key value of a democratic society. The rights and responsibilities given to all citizens of our country are evidences of this belief in the worth of each person. Universal suffrage, the provision of civil and federal courts, and free public education, all bear testimony to our belief in the value of every individual, regardless of his position or wealth.

Therefore: 1. *Teachers use positive ways of guidance which communicate this belief in the value of each personality, rather than negative ways which undermine self-confidence and self-esteem.*

Teachers do not use penalties or punishments which are personally humiliating to the student, or which destroy his self-respect. Shaming Johnny before the class seems to be effective—at the moment. Modern psychology and our democratic philosophy, however, are all against this method. Why? (a) It ruins the morale of the individual and of others in the group. (b) It destroys respect for authority as others feel resentment of the teacher's attack upon Johnny, or fear that they will be next. (c) The teacher shows by example that we do not have to respect others when angry with them. This method does not pay in the long run, since it diminishes the strongest motive for learning self-discipline—self-respect. Only as he views himself as a person who is acceptable and worth while does a person learn socially dignified ways of behavior. The teacher, therefore, considers the methods used in establishing and maintaining order against this criterion: Does the method show respect for the child's unique personality, or does it make him feel less worthy and of less value?

Therefore: 2. *Teachers consider each incident when discipline or order has broken down in relation to the particular persons involved, their needs and their life histories.*

Individuals are not punished as examples to the group. Because each personality is of value, in his own right, he is not used as a "lesson." Such a practice denies the uniqueness of individuals. Punishment—or a term which reflects a truer concept—the re-education of each child, must be based upon analysis of the causes of his behavior and consideration of plans suited to his own needs. When a child is used as an example, his attitude toward teachers' authority is disturbed and his confidence in their integrity is weakened. Those children who identify with the one being punished are apt to feel resentful or that the teacher is unfair. Other children, because of their own backgrounds and personalities, would never show the behavior which is being made a "lesson." These children often become so fearful and anxious that they are unable to behave spontaneously and constructively.

Study of individuals and the past events which influence their behavior, implies that schools must keep adequate records of students. Some people still consider the teachers' efforts to know each child as an individual a "newfangled idea," a new way of pampering the child. But only as each child is understood in the light of his own abilities and unique experiences can he be guided to develop the self-control and self-direction needed for democratic citizenship. The teachers' information about each student, and interest in him as a person, increase his self-respect and make him more educable for democratic citizenship.

Principle II.

As a nation we have confidence in the capacity of all to learn co-operation and mutual respect.

Our nation has shown the world that men can learn to live together and to reconcile their differing interests for the common good. In the beginning there were many who doubted that a government could be established without a privileged or ruling class. There were many who feared that "management," "labor," "landowners," or other special groups would seize control for their own advantage. At one time sectional interests did threaten the unity of our nation. At another period there was danger that the old country loyalties of new citizens might foment group prejudices and antagonisms. But in each crisis our national ideal of respect for every person and our dream of a good society have helped us develop ways of understanding differences and of working to harmonize them.

Therefore: 1. *Our schools provide a climate in which mutual respect and trust are possible.*

Young people learn to respect one another when they themselves have been treated with respect by understanding adults. Confidence in himself and others cannot grow when the child lives under a continual barrage of negative admonitions. It might be wise for every teacher and parent to calculate his daily ratio of positive as contrasted with negative comments. Persons who are dealt with in disparaging or humiliating ways very likely will learn to distrust all about them. Uncertain of themselves and suspicious of others, they are unable to merge their own interests in group goals. They fail to develop the cooperative skills needed to realize the ideals of our democracy.

Mutual trust also grows as people work together on problems to which each person may make a contribution. Initiative and self-confidence flourish as each child feels his importance in the group's endeavor. Teamwork and loyalty to one another develop as children begin to realize that each has a significant part to play for the satisfaction of all.

Mutual respect and confidence cannot grow when children are encouraged to vie with one another for a few prized rewards, or when children are assigned to spy and report upon one another. The questions may be posed: How often do our children in classrooms have even an opportunity to work on a group project? In what "group attainments" do they have a chance to develop pride? Is not the relationship too often between the teacher and each child, rather than a network of interrelationships leading to a sense of unity which includes the teacher as a group member?

Therefore: 2. *Teachers build understanding and communication between individuals and groups.*

The teacher's acceptance of each individual as a person helps children and adolescents to be comfortable with differences. All children are helped to know their own capacities and to develop their full potentialities. As they begin to understand their own strengths and limitations they learn to recognize and accept the abilities and needs of others. Differences in capacities and interests are recognized and valued in classroom activities even as our expanding industrial society utilizes an ever wider variety of abilities.

Within each classroom, too, there are generally wide differences in social background and life experience. Unless children and youth learn to appreciate these differences, without stigma, they become adults who are unable to understand or to communicate with those who are different. This is particularly undesirable in our country since wise self-government depends on our sensitivity to one another's needs and to our common interests. Through group discussions of their own experiences, and of those portrayed in literature, boys and girls are helped to see the universality of human needs. They begin to see why people learn to meet these needs in different ways and to express feelings in certain ways. They begin to see how family and social backgrounds teach us many ways of behaving which are neither good nor bad but simply different. Particularly in the social studies children are helped to understand why different groups in our communities have different purposes and how these differences affect our lives. As children accept differences they are better able to focus upon common, shared purposes and to learn how to work together upon common problems.

Principle III.

We believe in the right of people to have a voice in plans and policies which directly affect them.

In every phase of our national life the means by which more and more people may take part in decisions important to them have steadily extended. The right to vote on many issues—in the local community, the state and the nation—is an obvious illustration. Should our schools be consolidated? May we increase the tax rate? Who should represent us? The questions are put to the people. Continuously, too, privileges have been extended to more groups by removing racial and property restrictions, by including women, and by naturalizing the foreign born. Now, the inclusion of younger citizens and of those living in territories beyond the continental United States is being considered.

The right to take part in decisions, however, is not expressed only in legalistic or governmental sanction of the vote. In factories and on farms, in offices, homes and schools there are many evidences of this conviction that those most closely involved should be consulted. Decisions about conditions of work, a fair wage, benefits or awards, rules and standards once accepted as the responsibility of a few are more and more referred to the many.

Two important insights are back of this insistence that every member of a democracy has a part to play in arriving at decisions which affect him. One emerges from our experience that group decisions are often more trustworthy than individual decisions because the base of judgment and intelligence is broadened. Another principle is that as we share in making choices we learn to accept a responsible part in carrying out decisions or in changing them if they prove wrong. As a prelude to citizenship, children too must have practice in making decisions of meaning to them. Responsible citizens of a democracy cannot be developed through living childhood years in small autocracies at home and school.

Therefore: 1. *Teachers help children to understand the reasons for standards and rules, and to foresee the consequences of their own behavior.*

From the earliest years children are guided in formulating their own rules for living together in the classroom. The teacher indicates broad limits of acceptable behavior as each new class forms. Additional standards emerge, however, as the children, through experience, perceive that new rules are needed for more effective and satisfying work. This implies that there must be freedom to make mistakes, for it is the analysis of mistakes and conflicts that enables us to formulate rules and to internalize standards. Adults can, of course, foresee most of the problems which will occur as children work and live together in groups. Often they could plan in advance to avoid many of these problems. But such planning deprives children of the vital learning experiences which develop inner controls. As children experience the discomfort of spilled paint or mislaid books, for instance, they begin to see the necessity for agreements about order and placement of materials. As some anticipated activity is missed because of confusion in scheduling, they recognize the value of orderly procedures. Just as they learn that following the rules makes the game more fun for everyone, children with guidance are helped to formulate and accept the group regulations which protect them from their own impulses.

Therefore: 2. *Schools provide for children's growth in self-government through which they share increasingly in planning their own activities.*

Self-government is broader than merely the election of representatives who take action for the group. Self-government develops as children help to arrange the materials and equipment in the classroom, as they express their tastes in its decoration and in other ways make it their own. The ability to govern oneself grows too as children share in planning the day's work, make choices among several learning activities, and face decisions about their own goals and purposes. With increasing maturity children become able to shoulder more and more responsibility for the direction of their own learning and for the management of school life.

Principle IV.

We have trust in the rational approach to human problems and in the ability of human intelligence to resolve conflicts.

A democracy uses peaceful and orderly ways to solve problems and shuns the use of violence and coercion to effect change or to avoid change. With faith in collective intelligence we are accustomed to explore and test new ideas and to revise and extend many concepts.

Therefore: 1. *Teachers study children's behavior scientifically, searching for causes and formulating hunches and hypotheses about how changes may be made.*

Application of consistency, patience, and the intelligence, are essential in bringing about the changes in behavior which result in personalities fit for a democracy. For training authoritarian citizens, simple methods of coercion which bring about surface conformity in behavior may be effective. But for the more advanced and spiritual ideal of a democratic society one is bound to use the slower process which searches for causes, adapts environmental conditions, and encourages growth from within. Effective teacher-disciplinarians do not bluff or play God. They admit that they can make mistakes and that they do not know all the answers. But, by example, they demonstrate that solutions can be found and difficulties overcome as people work together.

Therefore: 2. *Teachers help young people to understand the reasons for their own and others' behavior, and to develop more effective ways of meeting common conflicts.*

Sensitive teachers use experiences throughout the curriculum as well as incidents of daily life to help children learn rational approaches to problems of human relations. In a primary grade, for instance, the teacher has read a story to her group of young children. Sally bursts out, "The girl was bad—she should love her little brother." But Tommy quickly responds, "The mother should pay attention to her and not just to the baby." As the children talk about the story the teacher encourages them to express and accept their feelings and to sense the feelings and concerns of others—the mother and the baby, as well as the child with whom they have identified. They begin to view behavior not as good or bad, but as reflecting their own feelings and as affecting the feelings of others.

A middle grade considering a problem of its own self-government offers another example. The safety monitor complains that Charles resisted his reminder and refused to follow rules on the playground, but Charles counters that, "He yelled at me and pushed me—he has no right to." Many of the children begin to take sides either with Charles or the monitor. The teacher asks, "In what different ways do monitors remind us of rules?" As children give suggestions they act these out, and Charles and others describe how each way made them feel. Thus, children begin to learn a variety of ways to play the role of monitor and to sense the effects of their behavior upon the behavior of others.

The question of educating for a democracy is not a choice between freedom and discipline. Only the self-disciplined person is truly free. The teacher, thus, helps children in learning to live constructively and harmoniously so that their individual drives are subordinated to their own ideals and to group welfare.

Ours has been called the "Atomic Age." It might more aptly be termed the "psychological age," as we earnestly apply what has been learned about human nature and its perfectibility to the day-by-day education of children and youth.

PART II

Discipline in Classroom Practice

ONE great task of the teacher is *to understand and accept principles of democratic discipline* and to guard against the demoralizing lure of long outgrown and primitive punitivism so successfully cloaked behind arguments of "toughness" and "realism." However, this is only one side of the picture. Let us not for a moment fall into the illusion that by understanding and accepting the principles of democratic discipline, we immediately move into a state of affairs in which all problems are solved, or will disappear. This is not so. On the contrary, administering constructive discipline is a more exacting task than taking refuge in a few simple punitive tricks. It is just as much more exacting and challenging as is modern medical thinking compared to the proud hocus-pocus of the primitive medicine man.

The other great task, therefore, which confronts the classroom teacher is *to translate the principles* of democratic discipline *into daily action* in the classroom. With this in mind the following aspects of the teacher's role are considered.

Teacher's Role in Educating for Self-Discipline

The Teacher—an Educator of Individuals. The responsibility of the teacher toward the "individual" and his rights and developmental needs is inherent in the concept of democracy. In Part I of this booklet we reminded ourselves of the tremendous progress made along this line during the past four or five decades. In times of strain we are likely to get excited about the problems we have not solved, and to forget about the things which have been achieved. So let us just point to these facts:

Research about human development in this country has compiled more knowledge of the individual and the way he grows, physically, mentally, emotionally, than has ever before been available in history in any nation.

Much of this knowledge has not been sufficiently organized; we are also behind in our ability to apply this knowledge. But the fact that such knowledge exists is something not to forget.

Psychiatry, psychology, mental hygiene and similar fields have helped us develop ways and means of studying the children we deal with, of organizing this knowledge for use by the educator on the job, of understanding and sizing up developmental needs of children that are not visible on the surface of classroom behavior.

Again, it is true that not all of these techniques have been worked out sufficiently well to be used profitably in all situations. But many are there, ready for use, and others are being prepared.

Teachers have become intensely interested in this singular chance to enrich their knowledge about the human beings they teach. Universities have had to modify their curricula to include more practical courses on guidance and personnel work than traditional fear of un-tried sciences would otherwise have suggested. In addition hundreds of teachers have formed groups in their own schools to share their knowledge and skills of child study.

It is true, of course, that much remains to be done. But it cannot be denied that more specific concern about the human child and what makes him tick is here to stay.

Some may check our enthusiasm at this point and say, "But listen, isn't it true that many teachers reject and despise the very achievements you seem so proud of here?" We thought so for a long time ourselves. However, after arguing with many of those who support these achievements, we have come to agree with them. Yes, it is true that many teachers reject the improvements we have made in individual child study as "sissy stuff" and "fads and frills." But do you know why they do so? Not because they do not see the value of all this, but because they get discouraged if you open up vistas for them and then do not give them a chance to apply what they see. For teachers, while invited or urged to become psychological, are still loaded with classes too large and with work loads too predefined to permit individualized work. It is the frustration of these factual limitations, rather than a lack of forward-mindedness, which causes most of the dissension and dissatisfaction.

On the whole, we think we have a right to be optimistic. We are far from having licked the problem of individualization, but as far as the American teacher's basic conviction goes we are on the road to making the challenge for individualized understanding a real issue in our school system.

In fact, in this respect we think the educator is better off than the clinical psychologist, for we teachers are not as pressed for time as are they—most of our children are known to us over a period of years. We do not meet the child in complete isolation from his natural life, but fairly close to it; so we can "get a feel" of the community of which he is a part while we go along. We do not work always in the shadow of such emergencies as delinquency or other maladjustments. So we can often "study" for a while in order to act with insight.

In short, as a nation, we have advanced tremendously during the past five decades along the road of individual understanding of the human beings we teach, even though much is left to be done in closing the gap between knowledge and actual application.

The Teacher—a Leader of Groups. However, we have tolerated a blind spot in our vision that causes us much concern. For while we were busy digging up knowledge about the "individual," we have neglected an equally important phase of our professional task. We might try to put it like this:

All this knowledge about the individual is fine. But—so what? We never work with the "individual" in mid-air; school classes are *groups.* The moments when a teacher deals with one child at a time in a consultation room are rare. The teacher's daily role is that of *a leader of groups.* It is true that teachers want to reach each individual child by what they do and by what they make the childen do. But *direct action is in and through the group.* Individuals are dealt with mainly insofar as they are embedded in groups, that is, as they are parts of some group pattern.

For a long time we did not know what this meant. Even now many people seriously think a group is just an arithmetical accumulation of so many individuals, and that the whole problem is one of numbers.

A study of group processes has revealed that groups are organisms of their own. Groups consist of individuals, it is true, but they are more than just so many people. They develop something like a personality, a "spirit" of their own; they develop some power within them, something upon which their functioning will depend a great deal, something that goes beyond the individuals who constitute them. In a group, for instance, whose spirit or morale is high, many an otherwise weak individual will be spurred on to better and more efficient performance. In a group whose morale breaks down, even individually well-meaning members will eventually become indifferent or ineffectual.

Leadership of groups is a task of its own, following special laws and peculiarities, a science in itself. The schools have had a vague awareness of this for quite awhile, but they have expressed this awareness in the wrong way. Some schools have tried to imitate blindly leadership techniques which were developed under other conditions, no matter how different the goal of their group may be. Others have conceived of the "group leadership" needed in schools merely as a managerial task of keeping a large mass of students subdued so they won't make life too uncomfortable for the adult.

There is no doubt that the managerial manipulation of group behavior remains one task basic to group life. However, this task is only part of and is not identical with the task of educational group leadership. If we compare not only our tasks but our chances for success with those of leaders of industrial groups or in the armed services, we must admit that we have reasons to be envious. Industry, for instance, carefully selects those who are fit for its purpose, and has an elaborate machinery available for this selection. The schoolteacher, however, is destined to deal with any group of children which the community presents.

Other organizations too have power to decide just how large an effective group should be and who should be sent to which group. Compared with this, the teacher is almost without influence. For decades educators have tried to convince the tax-paying public of the inadvisability of having groups of certain sizes, only to meet with financial objections or the suspicion of their being too lazy to do the job. There is little doubt that important social learnings are lost to many children as groups increase in size. Parents, teachers and administrators therefore must continue to work for reducing class size and toward alleviating crowded classrooms. Some difficulties which teachers face, however, are minimized as they become skilled in such group processes as organizing committees and providing for student planning and self-government. The particular composition of some groups also affects the control conflicts teachers face. When there is a concentration of children with personal problems, a group develops poor morale. Aggression may become highly contagious because the stabilizing influence of more normal children is lacking. Careful attention to the composition of classroom groups can make teachers more effective as group leaders.

In short, there is no doubt that many teachers work under tremendous handicaps when they are really interested in the art of group leadership. Good teachers, though, are used to these handicaps; so we do not worry that this statement will scare them away.

This does imply, though, that teachers need as much help in their task of effective group leadership as in studying the individual child. We also have to admit that we know less about group leadership than we do about the individual child. Research has let us down—it is only recently that scientific studies of group psychology have shown an increase in number. Psychiatry and psychology are getting interested in this area, but we are as yet poorly equipped to meet the problem of group behavior. Teachers, who have always wanted help in this regard, are still being fed with generalized statements instead of specific aids for the solution of problems, and many have trouble in seeing the problem beyond the point where it disturbs their own comfort.

However, we seriously think that we are making one step of tremendous progress because we are more than ever before aware of the task of group leadership. Awareness of a newly discovered task is usually accompanied by a lot of frantic behavior, hysterical prejudice and futile controversy. Thus some want to meet the challenge of group discipline by doubling the number of intelligence tests. Others want a "psychiatrist for every child," laboring under the illusion that problems of group behavior would disappear if every member of a group would be psychiatrized. Others use the newly discovered awareness of the need for group leadership to sell their special brand of punitive tricks to befuddled bystanders, or to cut out pages from the manual of "How To Use Night-sticks on the Beat" and glue it over the pages of "Education for Democracy."

We are, however, happy and proud to declare that we are not bothered by any of this. Any period of great discoveries is accompanied by the tomfoolery of scared hysterics, greedy charlatans, and hypochondriac gripers. The very existence of all this spectacle seems to us, the authors of this pamphlet, only a sure proof that something marvelous is happening, something that will wake all of us from a lethargic sleep.

Group Discipline—Need for Scientific Study. Education has not in the past given a sufficiently detailed answer to the problems of the teacher who wants to achieve good group leadership in his classroom. Many theorists have not produced any data-based insights on the basic mechanisms of group discipline. The classroom teacher on the job has been left rather alone in the process of achieving skills of working with groups. Well, then, let us forget about our theoretical disputes and get together on the scientific study of groups. Let us:

1. Find out the most frequent practical problems of group leadership which the classroom teacher on the job faces.

2. Find out the basic laws of nature about group behavior of growing humans (and we don't mean in general).

3. Make specific studies of the ways different leadership techniques affect certain types of group settings, by working with the teachers on their jobs.

4. Develop a body of well-documented and really practice-grown insights and criteria. These are not meant to make teachers conform to our personal convictions or creeds, but to be practical guides for them in the process of solving problems which arise within their groups.

It is the conviction of the authors that by getting together all of us can help produce something really applicable for the teacher on the job and that in the process of doing this we may forget rather than reinforce some of our outdated squabbles and stale controversies.

The Three Main Headaches

From our work with the practitioner on the job, it seems to us that the problem of group discipline constantly rotates around the following three thought complexes:

The Individual or the Group?
Managerial Manipulation or Attitude Change?
How Do We Know Whether "It Works"?

The Individual or the Group?

It is strange that when we face two good things, our first thought is usually: how we can sacrifice the one in favor of the other. For this is certainly the way the problem is usually stated in relation to group discipline. In theoretical discussions, most teachers could easily be split on this issue.

On the one hand, there are those who want to sacrifice the individual to the group. When any issue comes up, Johnny has to be put out because "his presence disturbs the group," or he has to be socked so as to "set an example" for the others no matter what this does to him, or he must be rewarded as an "example" to the group—even if this does transform him into a conceited snob and make the rest of the children envious. The defenders of this attitude obviously have a point, but when you ask them how far all this solves Johnny's problems, they do not like the question and tell you to be realistic or go home.

On the other side of the fence we find those who do not care much for the group Johnny lives in. Thus, they insist that you pamper the most sadistic child no matter how many others he harms. They demand that you give Johnny all the praise he needs to get along better at home, no matter how "unfair" you act toward the rest of the classroom. Or they insist that Johnny be given the classroom as a playground to use with complete license because this will make up for the frustrations he suffers at home. If you ask them, "But what about my group?" they do not like the question, and again say you must understand Johnny better.

The teacher with vision knows that both of these attitudes are silly, and that there is no way out but that of always considering both issues at once.

The group leader's problem is always to influence the behavior and growth of the individual, and to influence the behavior and growth of the group. These are the complications which teachers face as they try to maintain a balance between concern for the individual and the welfare of the group.

1. In certain instances of everyday group life, the one or the other issue may be more in the foreground. Some events of group life are more "group relevant" than others; other events bear more meaning in terms of the "individual case."

Example 1A: Johnny is at the stage of his development in which a lot of clowning is frequently used to gain group prestige. There is nothing really wrong with this. In fact knowing Johnny we are glad this is happening "at last." However, it is also usually unavoidable that children overdo this ambition at times and become so intense in their wish for applause that they disturb every serious teaching situation.

In this case it is *not* sufficient just to know that Johnny's behavior is all right, normal, understandable, even desirable from the angle of his own development. The teacher is still confronted with the job of limiting it, or else the whole teaching situation disintegrates.

Example 1B: The teacher notices that Mary is sitting back, obviously daydreaming. After awhile she finds that the child is seriously disturbed about some family situation. However, Mary's behavior is restricted to her fantasy life. She does not act in any way which would disturb the group or the teacher on the job. Her behavior remains, from a group angle, innocuous, though it is alarming as far as her own history goes.

In this case there is no *disciplinary* need for the teacher to interfere, but Mary's behavior is still an important educational challenge, for she needs help.

2. The techniques which will be good for the one purpose, to help individuals, do not always coincide with the techniques which are effective for the other purpose, to influence group behavior.

Example 2A: George is a youngster who does not respond readily to any non-autocratic approach. Appeals to group spirit do not mean much in his life, for he does not care much what the rest of the children think about him. What he seems to need at this moment is close supervision plus a very cordial friendship with his teacher. As long as this technique is used he functions fairly well. There are other children like him in the group, so the teacher decides she will work through this combination of benevolent autocratic dependence and personal love appeal. After awhile the group is exposed to situations in which the children ought to run things on their own. They are entirely incapable of doing so. For none of them has learned to act under anything but benevolent adult pressure.

Thus, the technique of benevolent autocratic friendship was right for some of the children involved, but it did *not* do the job of educating the group into a self-reliant unit.

Example 2B: The teacher has discovered that her classroom has deteriorated somewhat, has gone into a phase of being too wild for its own good, and is getting quite out of control. Instead of giving the teacher time to find out just what has happened and to go at the solution of this problem gradually, the principal insists that something must be done immediately.

Thus, the teacher decides to clamp down, sets up a few "examples," gets tough and becomes very suppressive and threatening in approach. This "works" as far as surface group behavior goes. The class begins to have a better record, produces less noise and is more submissive during teaching hours.

At the same time, however, some children in the class lose interest in schoolwork, begin to be late and truant, and neglect home tasks. Some attach themselves to delinquent gangs outside the school, even though they do become more submissive to discipline in school.

The technique of the teacher did work in influencing group behavior, but did not supply what these children *as persons* needed.

3. When there is conflict between the interests of an individual and the welfare of the group, one basic law may guide our disciplinary choice: the law of marginal antisepsis. By this we mean that a technique which is right for the child's problems must at least be harmless to the group. A technique which is rightly chosen for its effect upon the group must at least be harmless to the individuals involved.

Example 3A: Let us remember Johnny's problem in Example 1A. Johnny's clowning must be curtailed, or the group goals are too seriously hampered. However, now comes the question of *how* to change Johnny's behavior so that what we do is also harmless to Johnny.

Under ideal circumstances the teacher may plan to solve the group problem and Johnny's problem all in one big swoop. This the teacher might do, for instance, by really using a lot of time on Johnny, fixing up his home problem, finding him a nice boys' club where he can do all the clowning he needs without upsetting other people, having him psychoanalyzed, or by meeting whatever his special need may be. However, rarely are the circumstances as ideal as this. Often the teacher does not have this choice, cannot use as much time on changing Johnny's behavior and yet must get results somehow.

What our law of marginal antisepsis demands is that the teacher act at least in such a way that Johnny is not damaged. For instance, just punishing Johnny severely each time he clowns, or expelling him from school, would solve the group problem easily. But what would it do to Johnny, who now is not only without social approval but also more confused than before? Shaming him before the others might also do the trick as far as classroom behavior is concerned. But will this not take away what little social adjustment he has made and drive him into bigger and worse bravado before less sympathetic groups?

The cooperation of other youngsters in the classroom in helping Johnny understand the limits to which he can go will do the trick of checking Johnny's clowning, without making his own adjustment problem more difficult.

Example 3B: Ann is a youngster with a lot of inferiority feelings. The psychologist has advised the teacher that Ann needs approval and encouragement to regain confidence in herself. Consequently, the teacher goes out of her way to give Ann more praise than she deserves, and more directly and obviously than she would with other children. As a result, Ann simply blossoms for awhile. She is happy and proud

in class, more self-confident. The teacher thinks she has been successful in solving her problem.

However, after a few days this transpires: the other children do not
understand or even know about Ann's special problem. Thus, they are
bound to misinterpret the special attention she gets all of a sudden.
Thus they begin to distrust their teacher. They also begin to show her
what they feel. They become sloppy in fulfillment of their tasks,
gripey and grouchy about assignments. At last it ends with some of
the youngsters acting very fresh to the great satisfaction of the group.

The technique the teacher used to handle Ann's behavior was right
in the light of Ann's case history. However, the technique she chose
was bad from a group psychological angle. Uninterpreted preference
of one child's action before others may be misunderstood and may
release group jealousy and destroy group morale. Thus, the technique
was theoretically right for Ann's case, but wrong because it was *not*
"at least harmless" in its group effect. This does *not* mean the teacher
could not do anything at all for Ann, just because it would hurt the
other children's feelings. It does mean, however, that the teacher
would have to modify her plans, recognizing that she first needs to
help the other children understand the whole situation. Better still,
she may realize that she should have worked through the group to
begin with.

4. Contradictions which are unavoidable in any one moment of
group life can often be solved by *additional planning* for later situations.

Example 4A: The teacher is taking the children on a trip which
involves a boat ride. Naturally, they are in high spirits. She knew they
would be. That's why she took them on a trip to begin with. One
among them, Bob, apparently is a child whose self-control is much
lower than that of the other children. So the removal of usual be-
havioral inhibitions, while it makes the others just reasonably noisy
and mischievous, has too much effect on Bob. He becomes entirely
wild, unmanageable, acts in such a way that he threatens to upset
the boat.

Let us assume there is real danger involved. Then there is no doubt
that the teacher simply has to act. Even though she does not believe
in physical punishment and is not mad at Bob because she under-
stands, she will restrict him from upsetting the boat, even if she has
to hold him, or have the other youngsters keep him in line. This
"works" to the extent that Bob does not upset the boat. However, we

know that the emergency technique we had to apply is *very* bad and must have ill effects on Bob and the other children.

The moral of the story: we could not avoid doing what we did and, given the same circumstances, we would have to do it again. But we can avoid going home and thinking everything is all right just because the group effect we feared was avoided. We are going to:

1. Have a talk with Bob later and see whether we cannot help him to have more insight.

2. Make him see by the way we act afterwards that we do not dislike him simply because we had to stop his dangerous act.

3. Arrange for all-around planning which may make a more reasonable being out of Bob and which may involve manipulation of home and other relationships.

4. Or, in some cases, remove Bob to a group of children whose program does not include as advanced situations of free planning as that of the first group, which may be socially too mature for him. Which of these or other measures might be right will depend on Bob and his problem. What we want to point out here is that the necessity to do something on the spur of the moment which we know is wrong does not preclude our making up for such unavoidable mistakes by additional planning later.

Example 4B: Martha lives under most undesirable home circumstances. The teacher knows this and also knows what special strain the child is going through just now. Under the impact of all this, the girl becomes over-emotional and bursts out in a temper tantrum in the schoolroom, using rather wild language, even hurling insults at the teacher.

Ordinarily it would be the practice of the school to bring such an incident before the principal or to punish or at least reprimand the girl very severely, or to follow any one of the frequent practices of social ostracism or disapproval. The teacher realizes that the problem this child faces is so serious that it simply would not do to use any of these techniques or to call in the parents, or even to do anything which may make the child feel she has lost her last friend—the teacher. So she decides to make an exception. She does not react to Martha's insults at all, waits until the fit is over, then quietly goes over to the now crying child, and gives her all signs of undisturbed affection.

This behavior is just what Martha needed. Without it her case would have been unpredictably messed up. Yet the teacher also knows that this way of handling the case is not right in terms of the group as a whole. For she could not tolerate the same behavior by any child in the group just the same way, and since the other children know this, they must begin to hate Martha and become jealous of her and thus produce another problem for her on top of the ones she already has.

Still, the teacher thinks she acted right and would do the same thing all over again. Yet—she does not stop there. She realizes that something must be done to counteract the psychological mistake toward the group which was unavoidably involved in her behavior toward the individual. So she has a talk with the class, gets the children's frank reaction to what happened, lets them blow off steam against the bad behavior of Martha and even come close to criticizing the teacher for too much leniency. Then the teacher has a chat with all of them or a few—depending on the details of the situation—and explains that she has special reasons for acting as she did. This helps the group to understand and not to misinterpret her behavior toward Martha. She also leaves no doubt about her own criticism of Martha's behavior. She thus makes it clear to the group that she did not mean to ignore or condone what Martha did, but that she had other things in mind.

In summary we want to assure the teacher that we do not pretend that the problem of "individual and group" is always soluble, or easy to solve. We do want to imply, however, that in many more cases than we would think at first an adequate solution can be found if we are aware that good group leadership needs this double orientation all of the time. Such an attitude would help assure the fitness of what we do in terms of the individual involved as well as its group psychological effect. Many discussions which become a controversial either-or fight could be much more constructively resolved into a combination of these points of view, as we demonstrated above. Where the teacher is repeatedly faced with the situation in which a combination of these two viewpoints seems impossible, we can safely say that something is wrong with the way the group was composed to begin with. About this we shall have more to say later.

Managerial Manipulation or Attitude Change?

Another problem often confronts the teacher in planning group discipline. It is posed by the question—just what am I trying to accomplish? The purpose of any disciplinary measure can be geared in two directions, namely: (a) the technique can be planned to influence surface behavior right then and there; or (b) the technique can be charged with the task of influencing basic attitudes.

The alternatives offered here, by the way, may present themselves whether it is the individual or the whole group which we are trying to influence.

The following seem to us to be the basic principles underlying the "purpose" phase of group discipline:

1. Sometimes it is really important to manipulate surface behavior here and now, by any means. Failure to do so would constitute a serious mistake.

Example 1A: The teacher handles a class of rather disturbed children from a rough neighborhood in which vehement fighting is not socially rejected. At the moment her efforts seem pretty successful. The group is going fine and is obviously interested in the way she explains things which these youngsters had never grasped before. However, the group is an odd mixture of shy, withdrawing children and wild, close to dangerously aggressive youngsters with temper tantrums of long standing. While the teacher was busy doing her explaining, a little rumpus began to rise between two boys in the back row. In a group like this it would not do to pay attention to every little rumpus that occurs, or else the climate would have to be kept so punitive that no wish for learning or school acceptance could develop. Thus the teacher is used to ignoring little disturbances from time to time and has found that usually they disappear pretty well on their own. In this case, however, she is out of luck. One of the boys suddenly jumps up and pulls a knife on the other. In this case there seems little doubt in our mind that the knifing should be stopped, no matter in what way the teacher may have to interfere. Let us assume the boy is so upset that no mild form of approach has any effect; so the teacher has to hold his arm, take the knife away from him, yell at him, or even put him out of the room.

The importance of avoiding injury to the threatened child is sufficiently great to justify using any technique which is needed to bring about a surface change in behavior.

Failure to do so would be a serious mistake. It is needless to remind you that this constitutes only the first part of the real "handling" of this discipline case. Our examples in the previous section will easily point the way to more complete action.

Example 1B: The whole of the seventh grade is in an assembly with all the children of the elementary school. The second graders of this school have planned a performance into which they have put a lot of time and enthusiasm, and they have waited months for this chance to have their group applauded by the whole school. In this school the seventh is the highest grade. It is spring, the end of the term is not far away, and with it the end of all the seventh graders' stay in this school building—or so they hope. An hour before the program there had been a violent dispute about the outcome of a baseball game which had ended with a doubtful tie.

The seventh grade is not a bad bunch, on the whole. Today, however, they are insufferable. They behave so loudly and disturbingly in the assembly that the whole performance threatens to be disrupted. Miss Jones has a good rapport with her group, but today they seem to be in a mood when gentle interference does not last long. The only way to stop the trouble is to pull out the worst mischief-maker; then the others will wake up to the fact that she does mean business and will be all right for the rest of the performance.

In spite of the fact that Miss Jones knows that the loudest disturber need not be the real cause, that throwing the youngster out will neither change him nor really produce better morale in his group—out goes Bob who happens to be the first disturber after her last reprimand. The manipulation of surface behavior was her real task at this moment. Her technique was right and effective for her purpose.

Of course we hope she realizes the limitations of such techniques and will plan other things to meet the real problem later.

2. Sometimes it is really more important to reach basic attitudes by what we do, even though surface behavior does not change right away. To use a technique in such a case which does reach surface behavior but at the same time counteracts our deeper plans for influencing basic attitudes would constitute a serious mistake.

Example 2A: School System A establishes a "special class" for all those children who have become delinquent, especially for those who hate school and who feel that no one cares what happens to them anyway.

It is obvious that the only reasonable purpose which such a "special class" can have is to change basic anti-school attitudes. The "discipline" in such a class must be guided by this main goal all down the line. This means that the first task of the teacher is to show these school-suspicious children that she is "different," to stir up the wish in them to become identified with her, to accept her as "O.K." Miss Evans is well on the way toward succeeding in this respect. After weeks of careful study of these children and the way they are, she has figured out pretty well what behavior she must avoid so as not to be pigeonholed along with previous teachers who have marched past these children's lives without effect.

Last Monday two boys were caught smoking in the toilet. The teacher reprimands them for their act in just the way she is expected to as warden of school rules. But she avoids carefully the display of any moral indignation in talking about the incident, nor does she make an undue fuss about it. Later discussions with the children prove how excellently she has succeeded in gaining their confidence through her handling of this little incident. Thus, her technique was highly successful.

However, the rest of the staff does not look at the matter in this way. Miss Evans is openly called down for undermining the "discipline" of the school, is commanded to search each youngster for cigarettes before he enters the classroom, and to set up a reward for those who squeal. For so the reasoning goes—the repetition of smoking must be absolutely avoided.

As far as affecting surface behavior goes, the procedure recommended by the rest of the staff is right. Miss Evans' technique does *not* promise the safest insurance against the danger that another cigarette might be smoked in that school. A system of surveillance, spying and reporting might reduce the number of cigarettes smoked considerably more than would Miss Evans' technique.

As far as the real purpose of the school goes, however, the staff is wrong. The insurance of cigarette avoidance would demand techniques directly contrary to the educational goal which the school system had in mind in establishing this special class, that is, the change of the children's basic attitudes toward the school. By searching the members of the class, by offering praise for squealing, and by making a moralistic fuss about an undesirable but neighborhood-accepted behavior, Miss Evans would have lost all her chances for making any dent in the basic reaction of those children toward their teacher and what she stands for.

Example 2B: To be sure we are not misunderstood as implying that such considerations only count where "abnormal" behavior is involved, let us think of an ordinary school for normal children where it has been decided to experiment in self-government. Doubtlessly, such an experiment cannot be expected to add to the comfort of the adults, but has only one goal: to develop attitudes in the youngsters which will lead toward a growing understanding of the democratic process, the responsibilities involved in it, and the learning that is necessary to make it work.

What we have in mind, then, is the gradual learning of living to-gether within a pattern of self-government. We must realize at once that any technique which would promise 100 per cent "success"—meaning a frictionless life with no margin for learning from mistakes and developing self-reliance—would be obviously wrong. Entering upon such a project, we therefore understand to begin with (a) that the first phenomenon will not be improvement, but increased confusion as far as everyday routine goes, (b) that this confusion must *not* be avoided by autocratic interference, but must be exploited for a process of self-appointed learning from mistakes, and (c) that techniques which promise smooth functioning are *not* "successful" in terms of the basic job undertaken.

The success of the enterprise must be measured by the learning that was derived from the experience, not by the extent to which trouble was avoided while we went through it. Not surface behavior, but long-range attitude changes, are the goals in the light of which evaluation has to take place.

8. Most of the time we are really after both purposes: the manipula-tion of surface behavior, and the influence on basic attitudes. The difficulty is that some techniques are better fitted to produce be-havioral changes, others to bring about the change of basic attitudes over a longer stretch of time.

When confronted with this problem, we should again follow the law of marginal antisepsis. In this application the law would assume the following form: any technique used to bring about surface behavorial changes must at least be harmless to long-range attitude changes, and any technique used to invite basic attitude changes must at least be harmless to the surface behavior challenge we have to meet through reality pressures.

Example 3A: Mr. Morris goes out and gets himself some disciplinary advice. Tomorrow morning he will start a new regime. He sets up a rigid system of well-defined rules and regulations, merits and de-merits, rewards and punishments. The system is elaborate. It chal-lenges some students by its lures, frightens others by its threats; the results are unbelievable. Shortly after it has been installed, everybody has learned his task; everybody gets books and papers and well-sharpened pencils. The actual work and effort output has increased overnight.

We triumph too soon. We discover after awhile that the basic attitude of those children toward subject or teacher not only has *not* changed, but has deteriorated even further. They do not ask any more questions. They are not even confused any more about what algebra is good for—they have stopped caring. They do not fight their teacher's effort any more—they have come to despise him as pedantic, ridiculous, and "school masterish." They have no interest in the topic at all—they stall for time until the happy moment comes when they will not have to hear the word "algebra" any more. All that the new techniques have brought about is a skillful exploitation of our system so the youngsters will have less trouble while they go along. The real student motive is not to learn algebra, but to know just how to avoid too much friction with something whose meaninglessness they have come to accept as inevitable.

In short, the advice Mr. Morris was given from his disciplinary wizards was foul. He treated a lack of subject-related motivation with a candy-threat system for the manipulation of surface behavior. But he did not further—he even damaged—the long-range objectives he was hoping to achieve, those of gaining a group of children eager for the wisdom which he had to offer and acceptance of him as a person.

Example 3B: Miss Jones takes over an eighth grade. This class has built up a bad reputation and includes the worst hoodlums in the school. They and the less-delinquent children in the room are going through a period of vehement body changes and are obviously out of bounds. Things have become so bad that the whole school is in trouble because of them. None of the daily routine, including attendance or any type of work output is functioning any more.

Miss Jones has read a lot about "democratic procedures." So the first thing she does is establish a system of self-government. This has a few positive effects. The attitudes of some of these youngsters are better. They do not show so much obstinancy and spiteful rejection of school or teacher. But it is equally obvious that they cannot handle their affairs. Bullies develop who try to put the regime over on others but keep their own buddies tax-exempt. Rules are made and broken. Beautiful examples of learning take place in the discussions of group affairs, but the children still do not show any change in school attendance and work output, and they still get into everybody's hair.

The mistake is obvious. Miss Jones' idea was right to the extent that an experiment in self-government is the best way for youngsters to learn constructive attitudes toward each other and their community. However, we also know that such an experiment with a group that is not ready will not affect momentary behavior for quite awhile. In a camp her technique might have worked. With the school demands remaining what they were, though, Miss Jones' technique required a longer waiting time for changes in surface behavior than she could possibly have anticipated. Therefore, the technique was right in terms of basic attitudes, but was harmful because it did not solve even the minimum of actual surface behavior problems that *had* to be solved in this instance.

To be sure that we are not misunderstood, we had better add that there is no need in either of the two examples cited to swing over to the opposite extreme. In both examples we think a workable system of discipline which combines effectiveness in achieving one purpose with antisepsis in the other purpose could easily be suggested.

In both examples: (a) Some of the work could have been planned by teachers and students to encourage increased participation and meaningfulness which will prepare for deeper attitude changes. (b) Some parts of school life in each case could have been left safely to adult domination and interference without in the least jeopardizing freedom and growth in self-government in other activities.

In Example 3A, for instance, the algebra teacher could have made changes in his teaching techniques to bring algebra closer to the interests and the momentary needs of that age range and to develop increased participation by each student through group discussion. At the same time it would have been wise to establish some well-thought-out pressures and rewards to enforce certain work demands, without putting the whole weight of motivation upon these premiums and threats.

In Example 3B, on the other hand, Miss Jones could have made a sharp demarcation between two kinds of problems: those which the school will have to enforce, even though the children are not quite ready to see why, and those which can be safely opened up for free— and then *really* free—handling by the group itself. In this way the youngsters would have had a chance to practice how to be self-determining in activities in which they could afford to make some mistakes.

In summary we want to state again: we do not pretend that there is anything like a ready-made recipe, answering the question, "Just how much rope should be given for learning through mistakes, and which things do we have to insist upon because we cannot afford any concession in surface functioning?" It is obvious that we usually tend to err in either of these two directions. It seems to the authors of this book, though, that a careful evaluation of this whole issue of surface behavior versus basic attitude change would lead to many more satisfactory solutions than we can hope for without such a comparative study.

How Do We Know Whether "It Worked"?

If a group of people get together talking about problems of discipline, they have a habit of doing either of two things: they start a wild fight about "basic principles," pitching unsubstantiated belief against unsubstantiated belief, or they pretend to want to get together and become "practical" about it. With this statement they usually start on a binge of telling anecdotes. I have recently made a habit of analyzing such anecdotes about instances of good or bad discipline, about failure or success of punishments, about examples of how well physical punishment worked with John and how it wrecked his classmate.

There are two things all these anecdotes have in common. They all extol, with more or less of an attempt at disguise, the unique magical capacities of the personality of the speaker, and they are all on the level of primitive thinking as far as the criteria for evaluating why these tricks "worked" is concerned.

The following suggestions are guides for the practitioner on the job who wants to avoid being fooled by what other people pretend are their "experiences."

1. Claims of even the most brilliant experts that their techniques "work" remain meaningless for you until you examine those incidents in the light of the individuals you deal with and the characteristics of your classroom as a group.

Example 1A: Your ninth grade class comes from a highly conservative community with a lot of emphasis on Emily Post. The anecdote-speaker encourages you to create as much "informality" as you possibly can so that "the youngsters feel at ease and let their hair down." Watch out for that one. It all depends on just what the speaker had in mind when he mentioned "informality" and from which clientele his own experiences were gathered. Youngsters who are just moving into social strata a little higher than the one their parents lived in are often threatened by a return to the "informalities" of the group they left behind. An example is the deep aversion of Negro youngsters of the middle classes—children of white-collar workers who hope to become college students some time—for some youngsters of their own race who happen to indulge in zoot-suit rituals.

Example 1B: Your principal has called you in to find some way in which the noise and disorder in the study hall, containing as many as 350 children, might be reduced. The speaker in a meeting which the principal has recommended to you has just pointed out what a marvelous thing it is to abandon all rules, to let children learn from their mistakes, to develop a yearning for order out of chaos, gradually.

Unfortunately, he does not add that he is talking not about school but about a camp, not about keeping a study hall quiet but about keeping a camp cabin floor clean, not about an assembly room of 350 students but about a club group of eight.

Example 1C: Raymond behaved very badly in class today. He used a dirty swear word in front of you. You are uncertain as to just how you should handle this; so you ask the teacher with the greatest seniority to give you advice. This person knows the answer right away, and she speaks from long experience: "Let me tell you, my friend," she says, "you cannot afford to let this go unpunished. You must call the parents in. Then you must punish Raymond severely, or else all the other youngsters will start doing exactly the same thing."

While saying this, she remembers a scene with an over-developed bully of the knife-throwing variety in an assembly hall of sixty children, all on the verge of revolt, with the youngster's "gang" waiting to see just how the teacher would react. The situation for which the advice is given—*your* situation—is very different from this. Yet, your "experienced" friend does not bother about such minor details as the fact that Raymond is a shy and weak youngster, intimidated at home, that he adores you and happened to have this fit of temper out of "hurt feelings"; that Raymond's parents are cruel bullies who have no sense of proportion and discipline, who would either laugh at you for worrying about bad language, or would beat Raymond mercilessly, depending on how drunk they happened to be; that your classroom adores you, that they would "understand" if you wisely ignored the whole show, and that not a single one of them would ever dream of acting as Raymond did.

Example 1D: The children in your lunchroom labor under too many restrictions against noise and activity. They must only whisper, not talk. They must not move around, may not play table games. Every rule limits expression and is devised to keep action down. At the same time, your principal is worried about too many "explosions" in class. The other teachers complain that the children are restless and hard to keep in their seats.

You suggest that maybe, if you could give them a chance for some reasonable social contact during lunch period, they would not have to sneak in their chats with friends during class time; that maybe, if you gave them a happy recreation period in between, pent-up energy would be released and they would then be ready for quiet work in class.

One amongst your crowd jumps on you. "You are all wet," he argues, and he cites a case: "In the so-and-so school they tried it and it did not work. The kids just got rambunctious and went all over the place and could not be controlled any more."

This sounds like a "realistic" argument to begin with. But watch out for details. Upon closer analysis you would have found out this about the fellow's "example": The X children were of a different neighborhood altogether, bent on raising trouble and had a hateful attitude toward their school to begin with—yours are not that way at all. The X school experiment was not purposefully planned. It just happened that on the one day when the controlling teacher was not there things went wild. This situation is very different from the one you meant. The X school teacher, who complained that his youngsters went wild because of the freer lunch situation, did not know how to control children to begin with. They were always wild anyway, only this time he had a good chance to blame it on freedom in the lunchroom.

In short, advice is given from some specific situation which the speaker has in mind. The judgment that "it works" is meaningless, unless you know that your situation for which the advice is given is analogous in essential items with the one from which the advice was derived. Just such mistakes as this are responsible for the millions of cases where the "best of advice" does the "worst of harm."

2. Claims that certain techniques "worked" remain meaningless, until you know just what the speaker is talking about and the effect of his technique *on an individual child* or *on the group as a whole.*

Example 2A: You are worried about what you should do because Johnny seems to have become so spiteful recently and so obstinate in his behavior in class. Mr. Jenkins knows all the answers. He has it all worked out. He gives you a beautiful story of how he happened to be attacked by a youngster once, how he simply took him by the scruff of his neck and threw him out of the room, and "you should have seen the classroom after that. None of these kids misbehaved ever again." Thus, he strongly recommends scruff-of-the-neck seizure as the remedy for obstinate youngsters.

He does not even notice that he is talking about the effect of a technique on a group, while you wanted to know how to help Johnny change.

Example 2B: Dr. X of your school guidance clinic has it all neatly decided just how children who are aggressive in class should be treated by the teacher. He still remembers the case of George. George was so aggressive he nearly murdered a youngster once. Then he found a teacher who "accepted George," and from then on everything was in sweet harmony.

You try it with Ned—only it does not work. First of all, Ned gets only more aggressive as he feels backed up by your "understanding" —he happens to be a different type from George. Besides, Dr. X also forgot to check on another little matter. Even in George's case, which was supposedly such a success, something else happened which he himself was not interested in, but which you would not want to miss for the world. The children in George's classroom happened to hate George. When the teacher began to be upset about the way they fought him and began to defend him, they left George alone, but they picked on another youngster for a scapegoat. The technique suggested to handle the teacher's problem with Ned had implications far beyond its effect upon the individual in question. You want to help Ned *without* producing other scapegoats in class.

3. Claims that certain techniques "work" remain meaningless, until the speaker makes quite clear what he is talking about, namely, whether he means by "worked" a change in *surface behavior,* or a change of *basic attitudes.*

Example 3A: Miss Smith found a good trick of making her class "more peaceful." She simply told the children she would punish anybody who was caught in a fight with another child. She claims it worked beautifully and, with great gusto, recommends the technique to less-experienced colleagues.

The truth is that the children gave up open fights in class for realistic reasons. But they fought like cats and dogs outside of school. They simply kept a temporary truce for mutual protection while they were in danger. They were not "more peaceful" at all. So do not fall for this type of fraud.

Example 3B: Miss Jones just got a letter from Chuck. This letter is a singular document, illustrating what a teacher can mean in the life of a child. Chuck is in the service now, and has done a heroic act. The principal says Miss Jones can be proud of this letter.

Miss Jones can barely suppress a smile, for the principal was not around when Chuck happened to be the little boy she saved from delinquency. Things were different then. What Miss Jones did for

Chuck was not appreciated. It brought her the ill fame of being a sissy and a bad disciplinarian. The one outstanding thing in Chuck's life happened to be that Miss Jones was "different" from the teachers he had met before. He caught onto that once when he had been very mean to her in order to show off before the class. The teacher had failed to punish him, but had called him in for a talk instead. This talk is what he remembers now that he is far away in his country's service. At the time, however, Miss Jones was nearly fired by the board because her "techniques didn't work."

4. Do not allow anybody to say whether his techniques "work" or not, unless he is also ready to consider sub-surface effects.

Example 4A: In an institutional group, a poorly prepared counselor finds a beautiful way of "doing away with all swearing and bad language." He simply makes the children establish a rule that anybody who uses bad language is going to get a swat on his rear end. Bennie is appointed group executioner, and he "does a swell job." The technique "worked" 100 per cent.

A later study of the group reveals:

a. Bennie received bribes from half the group; so only a few incidents were reported.

b. Bennie beat up the rest mercilessly; so they had to do their swearing after they had locked themselves in the toilet.

c. Everybody began to hate everybody else after a while and to pick on each other mercilessly.

d. It all ended in a revolt against Bennie and in the group's refusal to hear of democratic self-government afterwards. The children distrusted their first experience in self-government because of its mismanagement.

e. Children in this group were found to be worse swearers than youngsters in other groups.

Still, while the subterranean effects of these techniques were un-x-rayed, their inventor could easily bask in the glory of having a "swell technique," the spread of which would solve "many problems of my colleagues."

Example 4B: "I do not believe in physical punishment myself, but George is a boy who really needs it. And it works swell with him. . . ." An examination of this claim reveals the following situation:

a. George has been cruelly whipped by his father ever since he was a little child.

b. George was put into this teacher's group suddenly from a very suppressive schoolroom. He did not understand that these children who also seemed to be from a more "refined neighborhood"—could submit to teachers without putting up a fight. So he began to brag how he "would show the teacher" and how he "could take it." When he was not beaten to make good his bravado, he began to ask for it more and more.

c. When he got his beating he was satisfied for the moment—things were as he knew they were: adults hated kids, and if you know how to get them mad it is worth while to take a licking from time to time.

d. George had put this teacher on the already large list of people who are just "adults to be fought." The teacher had lost all educational power over him for good.

e. Another teacher later met George. This teacher withstood George's temptations to be provoked. After much trouble the youngster all of a sudden realized that here was somebody who was different, who did care who he was, not only what he did. He then began to change.

Do you still agree that the first teacher's disciplinary trick "worked swell"?

Studying and Minimizing Discipline Problems

Three Types of "Discipline Cases"

The term "discipline case" is a beautiful example of a misnomer, for we obviously do not talk about a "discipline case" when we mean an example of especially well-functioning discipline, but rather when the very thing called discipline, i.e., "order," long since went out the window. If we can analyze what went wrong and what were the reasons that discipline or order broke down, we can better control and minimize these incidents. So-called discipline cases fall, as to their causative factors, into three categories:

Type I: Case History Produced. By this willful term we shall refer to the cases where it is obviously the peculiar disturbance of one individual child which causes all the problem.

Example: The principal asked us to go into the fifth grade and watch the teacher at work. He had thought she was a good teacher, but he had been forced to change his mind. He had sent Chuck, whom he knew was a difficult child, into her room because he had thought she might be good enough to handle him. Now he was disappointed and at the end of his rope.

Half an hour in the classroom left no doubt in our minds about the nature of the situation. It was *not* true that the teacher had handled Chuck wrongly. It *was* true, however, that her room was deteriorating more and more from day to day, and that the teacher too was at the end of her rope. The gist of the situation: Chuck is a seriously sick boy, to the point that he should be institutionalized, for there is no chance for repair without extensive psychiatric treatment. Chuck has lost all relation to anything that happens outside himself. His sudden "singing" or swearing has nothing to do with anybody around him, but pops up from inside fantasies without any tie to outside stimuli.

The teacher was a skilled person and would know how to handle a youngster who swore or sang out of mischievousness or spite. But in this case anything she did was bound to be wrong. If she put on the pressure that would keep Chuck even temporarily in check, she had to put on so much of it that the other children became afraid of her and mad at Chuck—the source of her punitiveness. Endless fights and squabbles were the result. If she ignored Chuck's behavior or approached it by the technique of repetitive interpretation, the failure of this approach and the tremendous patience squandered on Chuck were so obvious to the others that they hated Chuck out of jealousy and thought the teacher silly to tolerate such acts on his part. In short, Chuck was a pre-psychotic, so far beyond the reach of reality around him that he could not be approached by any technique within group life. He was the sole cause not only of the discipline problems he produced himself, but also of the bickering, dissatisfaction, hysteric over-sensitivity, and disorganization in his group.

The discipline problems developing in this group were obviously produced by the peculiar case history of Chuck.

Type II: Group Conditioned. By this term we refer to the discipline problems which are not the result of disturbed children, but of disfavorable elements in the *group*.

Example 1: Roy was the most outstanding "discipline case" of the year—a case of "sex behavior." The teachers felt they had to "set up an example." They eliminated Roy from their school system; so they obviously "had done everything they could to keep their classroom clean." The trouble was that in a few weeks another boy showed the same "sex behavior" in the same classroom; so the problem had stayed with them. Only the personnel had changed.

An investigation of this situation uncovered this condition of affairs:

Roy never was a real "sex case" to begin with. On the contrary, among the youngsters in the classroom Roy was about the most normal, happily growing, and well-adjusted boy. It was true, though, that he was older than the others, much more developed physically, and had first manifested sex curiosity a few years ago.

The problem lay with the rest of the youngsters, or the majority of them. They all came from families with an unreasonably strong taboo on the expression of any, even normal, sex curiosities in their children. At the same time these youngsters were just entering the stage of development when an increase in sex investigation is a normal rather than abnormal developmental characteristic.

Result: They were full of suppressed and over-heated curiosity, searching frantically for someone to nourish it. Roy, for his part, felt a little inferior to those children, for he did come from the wrong side of the tracks, and his academic background was not anything to brag about either. So he welcomed a chance to be "in with them," and to do some instructing on his part as a recompense for all the help on his homework he got from his more successful pals. When some of them were not satisfied with the harmless stuff he told them, he drew them some pictures—the only thing he was pretty good at —and their success led him on to more and more daring productions.

Roy's problem behavior is not the result of anything wrong with his case history. It is true that the overt "discipline problem" was focused around the person of Roy, but the actual discipline problem emanated from the problem of *the group* with which he lived. Not Roy's rejection, but a thorough and healthy approach to the group's sex curiosities by parents and school personnel would have been the answer. Since the latter was not sought, the *group situation produced another problem of the same variety* soon after.

Example 2: Miss Jones complains that "there is so much fighting" among her children that one teacher or another invariably sends in some complaint from the playground, the lunchroom, the gym, even the street—and it is always the children of her class who cause trouble. She adds that her children are pretty good as long as she is in the classroom, but that they are all "discipline problems" the moment she steps out.

Miss Jones was smart—she did not try to pin it on a boy with a bad reputation. She noticed to begin with that it was more than that, that it had to do with group morale.

An investigation revealed that the children were lured into good performance by attractive premiums for good behavior and by heavy punishments for even a whisper or a restless movement. After the hour was over, those whom she thought had sat still were highly extolled as pillars of virtue and offered to the others as worthy of imitation, while those who had not made the grade were exhibited as criminals, deserving of moral indignation and contempt by every righteous citizen in class. In fact, on several occasions Miss Jones had dropped unmistakable hints that she would understand, though not approve, if the virtuous ones would put an end to the misuse of friend-liness and freedom by the blacksheep of the group.

Result: All the suppressed body-restlessness of Miss Jones' hours with the class had to come out some place. Besides, all the inter-member furies and hatreds which piled up during those moralistic speeches of their teacher had to be translated into action at some time or other. In short, the undisciplined behavior of the various children sent in by other teachers in the school was not an outcropping of their delinquent case history, but was produced by the mistaken *group climate,* and would not stop until that atmosphere was changed.

In summary we might say that a large percentage of "discipline problems" in school classes are really of Type II, much more fre-quently than they are of Type I. These cases, of course, would not disappear even if we had "a psychiatrist for every child." For the trouble is not with the individual case history of the children, but with the psychological structure of the class as a group.

Type III: Mixture with Different Emphases. This type seems to us to constitute about 60 per cent of all discipline cases in school life. The behavior situation which creates this type of problem centers around some individual child. This child, however, is not a disturbed child of the extreme type; his behavior is produced by something in the group atmosphere in which he lives. Our problem in each incident is to define the *emphases* which must be put on causes in the in-dividual as well as group psychological causes. The remedy must consider both kinds of causes to the degree in which each emphasis is stressed.

Example: Don behaved so outrageously today that neither the teacher nor the other children in class can quite understand what happened. The teacher was investigating the alleged theft of a young-ster's purse from one of the lockers. It so happened that Don was seen near the locker and, in attempting to shed some light on the problem, the teacher first tries to identify those who were near. When she asks Don in the same quiet voice as the others whether he was around, he jumps up wildly, protests at the top of his voice that nobody is going to call him a thief and get away with it, and leaves no doubt in anybody's mind that he questions the legitimacy of that teacher's ancestral derivation. With this he runs out, tears bursting from his eyes, and slams the door behind him.

Since this behavior is quite unexpected to everybody in the room, it is easy for the teacher to keep her composure and to try and get at the source of Don's trouble right away. She turns her investigation of the theft into a discussion of Don's behavior with the class, has a talk with him after school, and unearths the following data:

1. Don had an unfortunate experience exactly a year ago. Some youngsters in the school which he attended tried to pin an incident of stealing on him. His very strict, irascible, and opinionated father exposed Don to a severe beating without even investigating the truth of the accusation, and did not even find it worth while to say something along the line of being sorry for his mistake when he later found that Don was innocent.

2. Don had not only a very strict and autocratic father at home, but had the bad luck of running into opinionated autocrats in his school career, too. Don's present teacher seemed like a miracle to him. He had met her with distrust, but was now just at the point when he was ready to admit that at last he had found a human being who was willing to stretch out her hand to him, no matter what people said. Then, all of a sudden in hysteric over-reaction to her question, he thinks that maybe she is just like all the rest.

3. The group, too, had been nicer to him than previous groups of children. He was eager to be accepted by them, wanted to be "one of the family," as he had never wanted that before. The idea of being "suspected by the teacher in front of all the others" made him see red.

Needless to say, this teacher had an opportunity to solve the problem without any fuss at all because her analysis had unearthed the most vital factors involved. Here is what she did to meet the problem: she explained to the group, in Don's absence, that she had talked with him and had found out what upset him so much. While she could not divulge the content of her conversation, of course, she knew the other youngsters would accept her judgment that it was best to make no further issue of Don's behavior. She and Don would clear it up together. She also had a talk with Don, showing him she understood and preparing him to return to the class.

The analysis of the incident shows that part of the problem is connected with Don's personal history and can be understood only on that basis. However, it also shows that another part is related to the group role which the teacher played in helping Don adjust himself to the other children and find his place in the group. The handling of the discipline case, therefore, demands an approach in the direction of both case-conditioned and group-conditioned elements.

According to our experience, we would dare to make the following generalizations:

Only about 10 per cent of all cases of school discipline are due to "individual disturbances" clear and proper. About 30 per cent at least are cases where problem behavior is produced entirely by group psychological inadequacies of school life. About 60 per cent of the cases seem to us to involve both personal case history of the individual and some deficiency in the psychological structure of the group. This means, then, that at least 90 per cent of all discipline cases are in dire need of group psychological analysis and consideration.

Prevention of discipline problems, then, must involve a quite extensive job of group psychological engineering.

What Most Frequently Goes Wrong in School Groups

At this point a thorough analysis of a wide variety of discipline cases should be presented. The group psychological factors involved in them should be carefully carved out and multiple choices for solutions should be suggested. However, such an approach—the only one that would be of really practical use for the teacher on the job —cannot be made in the limited space of this study. Nevertheless, we shall at least try to enumerate the most frequent types of group psychological factors contributing to discipline problems. We have to leave all interpretations and applications to the reader's own imagination, but hope that we may be able to follow this presentation with more concretely helpful illustrative materials at some later date.

Remember—our thesis is this: many discipline problems are not the result of something wrong with the individuals involved, but are the outcropping of factors in the structure of the group in which the individual lives. When something is wrong with the group in which an individual lives, even the most normal individual is likely to produce confused action leading into problem behavior. What we are investigating now is just what it is that most frequently goes wrong with school groups, and, therefore, constitutes the highest disciplinary risk. We think we can group the results of our analysis under six main factors:

1. Dissatisfactions in the Work Process

The fact that bad teaching or poor curriculum planning automatically increases the number of discipline problems has long been recognized. Indeed, for awhile we placed so much emphasis on this that we regarded it as the only source of discipline problems. There are still some who adhere to this assumption, loudly protesting that a teacher who knows how to teach won't have any discipline problems in her classroom. This is a wild exaggeration of an otherwise very worthwhile principle. Exaggeration in the opposite direction can also be heard from time to time, namely, that discipline is due only to "personality factors," "mental disorders in the pupils," and that it has practically no relationship to the curriculum as such.

Rejecting both extremes and trying to salvage the morsel of truth contained in both, we would like to suggest that *any disturbance* in the satisfaction children get out of the work they do with their teachers is likely to reflect itself in the *production of problem behavior*.

Subject matter much too easy. Too much of the work ability of the students remains unchallenged and has to search for other outlets.

Subject matter much too difficult. The emotion of frustration accompanies great stretches of the work. Research has proved beyond doubt that exposure to the frustration of not being able to do things well will produce tremendous aggression or restlessness in *normal* children. The result will be unavoidable diversions, taking pokes at each other, dropping and throwing things, irritability, and I-don't-care attitudes, which lower behavioral inhibitions.

Language of teachers too remote from the child's developmental level, or from the native tongue ordinarily used on his social plane. If that is the case, the child feels out of place, not really wanted, or even looked down upon, and begins to show signs of social-outcast reactions and protest.

Load of assignments too heavy. In this case the school hour is loaded with the emotional strain of guilt feelings, criticisms, and a general impression of not being up to what is expected, or an attempt is made to catch up on lost play time by having a good frolic during class.

Load of assignments too light. Then the feeling of progress in learning is lacking, which is reflected in a growing unwillingness to do any work because the time spent does not seem profitable.

Assignments badly planned, poorly explained, unfairly judged—with the result that typical "resentment behavior" pops out in little irritations.

Type of work or way of presentation too advanced—not clicking with the developmental needs of the children. For instance, lectures on nature in general are given at an age when a strong curiosity about animals' bodies could easily be used for motivation.

Type of work and presentation too infantile, compared to development level on which children move emotionally. For instance, talks about sex and the flowers are too childlike, when youngsters are full of pride about their newly acquired pre-adolescent daring in sex exploration on a very different level, indeed.

Activities too much on a merely verbal level, leaving the normal motoric needs of growing children unchallenged for long stretches of time. Thus, we frequently find restlessness, noise, shuffling of feet, falling of chairs, and pushing each other where too much discussion or lecturing substitutes for real participation and manipulative activities.

Work badly scheduled in its sequence, or ill-placed in terms of exhaustion and fatigue. For instance, English poetry is read at the end of a long day after a baseball game, at which moment it seems to be especially hard to excite manipulation-greedy sixth-graders about Shelley or Keats.

The examples could be multiplied by the hundreds. Suffice it to say in summary that any serious mistake in curriculum planning or failure to relate it to the real growth needs of children and youth produces discipline problems, even with the most normal and well-mannered group of youngsters. Boredom and fatigue are known to be the worst enemies of school morale. Only the most deficient children do not care whether we bore them or not—they apparently fail to notice or care what happens around them anyway. Normal youngsters will spontaneously search for substitute satisfactions if taught the wrong way. This natural self-defense by the normal individual will present itself as a "discipline problem" at times.

2. Emotional Unrest in Interpersonal Relations

The schools were originally designed as places for learning. Unfortunately, we do not invite only the various I.Q.'s of the children to come into the school. The youngsters bring, often to our great discomfort, other parts of their personalities as well as their intelligence. They bring perceptions, moral attitudes, and whatever else needs to be taught. They bring their bodies—and every part of them, no matter how disturbing or unnecessary for what we want to teach. And they bring the whole inventory of all the emotions they use at home and on the playground, as well as those which are relevant to the acquisition of wisdom and knowledge. No wonder they also "live" in our classrooms, whether we like that or not. This means that they form attachments and hatreds, cliques and sub-groups; they hope, love, hate, and fear. They experiment with each other as potential friends, sweethearts, rivals, cooperators, bosses, even slaves.

They try to experience the whole scale of person-to-person relationships with which they have become acquainted in their private
life. In short, life goes on in spite of the curriculum plans we may have.

Conflicts arising from personal relations will be reflected in "discipline problems." Such discipline problems are often not even directed
at us at all, but they are there just the same.

Individual friendships and tensions. Strong, sudden friendship among
youngsters sometimes creates "stubbornness" or "resentment" against the
teacher who is seen as an intruder bringing criticism or blame. Vehement
antipathies, hatreds and animosities between youngsters may interfere with
reasonable adjustments to the teacher's demands or to work interests. Sometimes even work and achievement become only one symbol of this tension
among individual children. Instead of being a serene process of intellectual
growth achieved in emotional isolation, education takes place in an arena of
strong and often conflicting interrelationships.

Cliques and sub-group formations are often the backbone of group life,
the greatest pillars of learner-morale. Sometimes, though, they may confuse
the school picture no end. Thus you may get sub-groups set against each
other, so that anything you say becomes unacceptable to group one just
because it is so enthusiastically received by group two. Or you may find
that various sub-groups begin to impress each other by the degree to which
they vie for or rebel against your leadership.

Many fights and instances of undesirable behavior are an expression of
such sub-group tensions, rather than a direct attack upon the order you
represent. Such sub-group formation may take place according to similarities
in developmental age, sex, or degree of sophistication. Some groups are
formed because of social discrimination or racial or national differences.
Others are drawn together because of academic interest, their liking for the
teacher as a person, acceptance of school code, and many other reasons.

Disorganization in group roles. Every teacher knows what "group roles"
are although the term may not be familiar. A few examples may show the
phenomenon. Almost any classroom has one or the other of such typical
functions as leader, second in command, organizer (with or against the
teacher), janitorial assistant, teacher's pet, model boy, blacksheep, scapegoat, bully, isolate, rejectee, group executioner, attorney-at-law, defender
of the innocent, group clowns (with or against the adult), hero in battle,
fifth columnist as to group interests, seducer and ring-leader, trouble starter,
rabble rouser, appeaser, humorous rescuer of tense situations.

Whenever any one of these roles is badly filled or not needed although
a lot of individuals strive to establish themselves in such roles, or when
many youngsters fight for the same group role, you are likely to have a rise
in your discipline problems, no matter how nice these youngsters or how
smart you yourself otherwise may be.

Pupil-teacher frictions. The fact that strong frictions or emotional disturbances in the feeling of youngsters toward us are the source of many discipline problems has long been recognized in theory. Often, however, we
are not quite aware of the degree to which pupil-teacher emotion enters the

production line of discipline problems. For often these emotional elements are of low visibility, and sometimes even the youngsters themselves are unaware of their existence or deny them loudly to others and themselves. The most serious producer of discipline problems is the trend of so many youngsters to project upon the teacher underlying attitudes developed toward the family at home. Thus, strong feelings of youngsters' "not being liked or understood" or of "being discriminated against" frequently may be expressed although a real mistake has not been committed in school.

Any tension, conscious or unconscious, existing among the youngsters is likely to color your classroom discipline. Especially in cases of general irritability and touchiness or widespread "uppetiness" and resistance on the part of whole classrooms, the suspicion that some of this goes back to disturbed interpersonal relationships is frequently justified.

3. Disturbances in Group Climate

Without an opportunity to define "group climate" adequately we can still put across what this term means by describing instances; for teachers experience group climate all through their work, even though group psychological discussions have been kept out of their teacher-training curricula. On the whole, we mean by this term the feeling tone which underlies the life of a group, the sum total of everybody's emotions toward each other, toward work and organization, toward the group as a unit, and toward things outside.

The punitive climate is one of the most frequent distortions of climate in classrooms. A punitive climate is not identical with "a case of punishment." On the contrary, wise punishment usually does not at all imply a punitive attitude by the teacher toward the child. On the other hand in a thoroughly punitive climate the pressure on children is often so continuous that the teacher need make only sparse use of actual punishment.

However, the punitive climate is perhaps the most destructive of group morale and discipline. It invariably produces these characterological side effects: the teacher shows little respect for the persons in his room, being so sure they can be managed by threat and fear; the pupils usually expect absolute acceptance or rejection according to their adoption of the teacher's behavior code; they usually fall into two groups—some rebel, hate, and fight back (the open "problem cases" in a punitive group), others identify themselves with the teacher out of fear and, therefore, have to become moral hypocrites in their attitude toward the other children. They are suspiciously submissive as long as the teacher is present, squeal on neighbors when they get a chance, and, in general, develop a holier-than-thou attitude. The emotion of fear of reprisal and shame is in the air most of the time, the teacher as well as the onlookers obtaining chronic sadistic enjoyment.

It is this kind of climate that breeds sadists, bullies and hypocrites. In this type of group it is a sign of character and courage to become a behavior problem. The morally healthful individual is the most frequent victim of the punitive climate.

The emotional blackmail climate is another distortion of healthful group living. It is a variation of the punitive climate but in a different disguise. In the emotional blackmail climate the teacher "loves" all children and says so at the rate of three times a minute. At the same time she rubs it in about how nice and unaggressive she is—how she will never punish anybody for doing wrong—while she drips with enjoyment of the self-induced guilt feelings. In the emotional blackmail climate, you do not get punished if you do wrong, but you know you have to feel like a heel for three weeks afterward. The teacher in this climate produces a tremendous emotional dependence, exploiting it as the only source of influence.

The results of this type of climate are these: a surprising absence of physical or other obvious violence between teacher and children, often confused with understanding and progressiveness in technique; an extreme fear of the teacher's disapproval, resulting in extended orgies of self-accusation by the children and hurt feelings by the adult leader after each disciplinary breach; a strong rivalry among some of the "good" children with those who are not as emotionally close to the teacher as they.

The discipline problems of this group will be especially strong when these children move from younger childhood into early adolescence when so much adult dependence is unnatural. The main casualties of this climate are those who want to grow up and become independent and would rather take the rap for a mischievous act than turn into self-depreciatory introverts at the teacher's command.

The hostile competition climate. The hostile competition climate is a distortion of an otherwise wholesome phenomenon in our society. Normally, a good deal of competitiveness is unavoidable and even liked by children growing into a society where there is little doubt of the presence of competitiveness. However, there are two things that can go wrong with a normal competitive climate; one is that there may be more competitiveness than children need or can stand without developing negative character traits or defeatism; the other is that competitiveness may deteriorate into hatefulness.

The hostile competition climate can be characterized thus: everybody is whipped into aggressively competing with everybody else all of the time. Reward is given to him who proudly tramples under his feet anyone who dares to compete with him. Shame falls upon the head of the child who would rather get a lower grade than feel holier-than-thou toward his best pal. The hostile competition climate turns a classroom into a dog race. It is highly doubtful that mutual love and friendship are instigated in the participants while the race is going on.

Results: Extreme uncooperativeness among group members so that all organization has to be enforced by outside rules and pressures. Those who happen to be last in the line of aggressive competition become outcasts. Snobs develop from those who happen to hold the front line easily and get ten times the praise that their efforts deserve. The result is that such groups depend on autocratic management with no real wish for democratic cooperation and self-management. They come to enjoy punitive instances of discipline as an outlet of all the hostility and moral snobbishness fostered undercover.

The group pride climate has a very wholesome counterpart. What we mean here is the distortion where the group leader tries to develop a strong emotional relationship in every member toward the total group, and then overfosters a feeling of vanity and conceit related to the group. Good "teams" sometimes allow their team spirit to disintegrate into this climate.

The group pride climate usually develops a high degree of group consciousness in a classroom resulting in many positive attributes. At the same time it produces a host of potential executioners who wait for a moment when they can swoop down upon the unlucky devil who was a stain on group honor or reward. It develops a set of chronic rejectees and releases wild mob-lynching psychology against them under the cover of righteous group indignation. Violent fights or the chronic problems of the constantly persecuted and despised rejectee are the main discipline problems engendered through this climate.

We could—and should—continue this analysis of typical classroom climates. Suffice it to say here that the total climate which governs the social relationships among teacher, children and total group has a tremendous influence upon the type of discipline problems which will be automatically avoided or automatically produced. We also admit, though, that this factor along the production line of discipline problems is as yet the most difficult to analyze without further group psychological instruments.

4. Mistakes in Organization and Group Leadership

Many teachers do a perfect job of teaching, as far as the presentation of subject matter and the organization of learning experiences go. They also have a fine teacher personality and a very fair approach to "the child." Where they get in trouble is in the mechanics of group leadership. For the successful handling of groups is as complex a task as the organization of subject matter.

Since teachers receive practically no organized training in group leadership, children are exposed to a hit-and-miss technique that causes many problems which could easily be eliminated. Again we shall have to select only a small fraction of possible illustrations.

Organizational Mistakes

Too much autocratic pressure, especially at ages where gradual emancipation from adult leadership is a natural and important trend. Program and organization become so adult-centered that there is little feeling of real and meaningful participation by the members of the group.

Too little security given the group by adult leader, leaving the children constantly exposed to the strain of self-responsibility and moral guilt. Tossing all responsibilities over to the group with little reference to the children's developmental needs or emotional maturity is often mistaken for "self-government" and "education for democracy," which it certainly is not.

Too high or too low standards for group behavior. The first mistake exposes children to moral defeatism resulting in irresponsible mischievousness as a way out. The second mistake gives them no chance to satisfy a normal amount of "group pride." As a result they get disgusted, disgruntled, develop a feeling that their group life is childish, is not worth while, and they show such reactions as boredom and fatigue.

Too much organization, life regimented by a thousand silly little rules which you bump into wherever you turn. As a result, trouble-avoidance is likely to take the place of really serious group-mindedness.

Too little organization so that all issues have to be decided on a moment-to-moment basis and the children never quite know what to expect.

Group organization out of focus with age, developmental maturity, special type of background, or specific needs of the group. This is especially true where schools change their clientele. For example, when new boundaries are set up for a school, families of different ethnic and socioeconomic backgrounds may replace a hyperambitious, overprotected group from a "refined" neighborhood, while teachers and school organization maintain the same basic disciplinary pattern. Constant revision to fit organizational patterns to total school structure and needs is essential.

Personal Mistakes

Lack of tact, especially frequent with the highly ambitious and subject-matter-minded teacher who has little imagination about how children feel. This characteristic is especially frequent, also, in the transition from one developmental phase to another, when teachers sometimes try to treat a youngster as though he is much younger than he feels.

Indulgence in personal sensitivities and allergies, superimposing one's own personal behavior code on the children regardless of whether it fits. For example, tremendous sensitivity to language with pre-adolescents from a low protection area, or extreme touchiness about personal vanity with children who have little school-mindedness or adult-security at home.

Over-reaction to dignity violations. Many apparently serious discipline problems have little at all to do with actual discipline. Such problems may reflect the hysteric reactions of an oversensitive adult toward irritating child behavior, especially when there are differences of social background and manners.

Plan for revenge instead of educational change. To "show them" or "give them what they have coming" is often made the prime motivation of the way discipline problems are handled, while the chances for a real change in the child's attitude should be the only thing that counts.

Inconsistency in promise and threat, if extreme, undermines group security and gives children a feeling of unpredictability against which they rebel or because of which they may develop defeatist attitudes toward all group issues.

Stupidity in carrying out promises or threats. The idea that consistency in itself is a virtue and that it is better to be consistent and do the wrong thing than ever change one's decision, is likewise a serious mistake. Children watch the thoughtfulness with which you plan your action. Thoughtfully documented change of decision is more respect-creating than silly, stupid or inconsiderate sticking to the wrong guns.

Wrong use of punishment and reward, reasoning, interference, or "learn by mistake" techniques. Obviously wrong applications of any educational techniques undermine group morale and develop "try and don't get caught" psychology. What constitutes "wrong use" is, unfortunately, too involved to be opened up here, for the "wrongness" must be judged in relation to the child's impulses, what has happened before, and what the immediate conflict means to him.

Wrong arguments about educational techniques. More children disobey because of the silly arguments on which obedience is sold to them, than out of opposition toward obedience itself. In talking to a group, teachers are likely to support the right things they do by the wrong arguments, and thus produce resistance where there was not any to begin with. This is especially true during early adolescence, where the group code of children changes so that the same argument that would have appealed to them a few years ago is that much provocation now.

Mistakes in emotional distance and proximity. Such mistakes are known to be factors in undermining group morale. Emotional preferences and rejections may be noticed by children even though we may not be aware of these ourselves. Emotional inequalities of reaction based upon social class, ethnic or racial differences are special dynamite.

It would be easy to extend this list further. Let us summarize briefly, however, by repeating, even with excellent teaching ability guaranteed, even with a fine attitude toward "the child" at the outset, any mistake in the organizational or personal management of groups is likely to produce problem behavior in children. An evaluation of group leadership techniques which we use is essential from time to time. Children as well as the world around them change more rapidly than any list of generally recommended, previously practiced educational tricks.

5. Emotional Strain and Sudden Change

Emotional strain, affecting a whole group, may in itself be sufficient to produce upsets and problem cases. We know this is true whenever the emotional strain on groups is easily recognizable as such.

The state of *anxiety* which many school groups experience for weeks during "examination period" and while waiting for the results, is a frequent example of group strain. In the same way, sudden effects, which may sweep classrooms at times, are productive of unexpected problem behavior. Excitement about such a contemporary event as a community riot and resulting emotions of extreme fury, enthusiasm, unusual hilarity, as well as depression and fear, are among the prime dangers to stable morale. Needless to say, constantly whipped up excitement and aggression in time of war work as chronic irritants to the discipline of many school groups and add unnotice-ably but considerably to the problems of the teacher as a group leader.

One of the most outstanding deteriorating effects of emotions upon group morale, however, does not flow from wild acts and excitement, but rather from the lack of it over too long a time. Boredom will always remain the greatest enemy of school discipline. If we remember that children are bored, not only when they are not interested in the subject or when the teacher does not make it interesting, but also when certain working conditions are out of focus with their basic needs, then we can realize what a great contributor to discipline problems boredom really is.

With classes too large, part of the children will of necessity be bored, while others may enjoy what goes on. Rarely can any one teaching procedure be exactly right for everybody. Another form of boredom in classrooms comes from an overemphasis on verbalization, while the manipulative needs of children are left unattended. The reverse—prolonged manipulative ac-tivity leaving the imagination no chance—may also bring on boredom.

Research has shown that boredom is closely related to frustration, and that the effect of too much frustration is invariably irritability, resulting in withdrawal or revoltive opposition or aggressive rejection of the whole show.

Reaction to change is perhaps the most frequent and, as yet, un-recognized factor in discipline difficulties. Of course we would expect such an effect from changes for the worse. It should be kept in mind, however, that any change, even a change for the better, tends temporarily to upset group organization and lead into a phase of increased problem production.

Many teachers will remember how even their nice classrooms are some-times hard to manage when the usually light room is darkened, when the lecture setting changes to discussion, subcommittee arrangement, or picture-slide demonstration; how much noise and confusion often accompany changes from one room to another, from class to luncheon and the other way around; and how otherwise very studious children may suddenly act very foolishly in the museum they wanted so much to visit.

The change in group leadership weighs heavily, too, in reaction to change. Much of the trouble substitute teachers have with classes has little to do with the real quality of those classes or with the teachers' actual ability for group leadership. For, when you meet a class not with its constant leader, the class has already deteriorated into something more akin to a mob than a group, and the task of leadership is very different than it would be in normal conditions.

Changes in program affect groups the same way, and especially changes in leadership technique. The most frequent example of this kind of change is the attempt to spring self-government unexpectedly on a school. What you will find during the first few months will have nothing to do with the children's reaction to self-government. It is only the reaction of the children to the fact of change itself. Only after a few months will their real reaction to self-government, their ability to take it or their immaturity toward it, become visible at all.

The answer to all of this, of course, is not that change should be avoided at all costs. The answer is that the knowledge of this law of group psychology should guide us in our evaluation of what happens and that we sometimes can meet confusion caused by too sudden change through planning for it by means of "transition techniques."

6. The Composition of the Group

The problem of "grouping" has never been satisfactorily discussed —to say nothing of solved. The most frequent controversial disputes are concerned with intelligence versus maturity grouping. Unfortunately, neither of the two is a way out. The real picture is much too complex for that.

Without entering into this very important and devious problem here, we can generalize safely to this extent: whenever something is very wrong in the composition of a group, discipline problems are the natural and unavoidable result.

If this is true, then the discovery of just what constitutes healthy divergencies as compared to serious mistakes in group composition must become of prime importance.

The following principles can be suggested without too much risk:

1. The question is not whether groups are heterogeneous, but whether or not the *criteria* in which they are heterogeneous are relevant for group life.

Example 1A: The tenth grade is well matched as to interest in and ability for Spanish although very divergent in developmental age. Some of the students are wildly adolescent, others have in many ways left their adolescence behind them, still others are just in the transition from a delayed childhood.

Result: Since they were all picked because of their interest in and ability for Spanish and since the Spanish teacher does a superb job of teaching and group leadership, they are a happy group for the Spanish class in which they are together once a week.

This class would be in complete chaos if the youngsters were expected to live as a group for even one day in camp.

Example 1B: The children in Cabin 8 are of quite varying I.Q.'s. Yet, they are well matched in camp interest, degree of sophistication and developmental maturity. So they make a superb cabin group, in spite of the fact that it would be nearly impossible to teach them any one academic subject because of their wide individual differences.

2. Every group is always badly matched in some criteria, even though it has been well matched in others. The real problem, therefore, is to avoid extremes in those criteria which are "marginal" to the main purpose of group life.

Example: The Spanish class mentioned earlier has one mistake in its organization. There are only three of the children who are very immature in their outlook on life and sex. The more sophisticated ones are so in the majority that these three are very much out of place. We will observe that after a few weeks of concentration upon Spanish, the three immature children will become problems. They will be either fearful of expressing themselves, or they may become clownish and wild in their attempts to impress their more sophisticated companions. Thus, the too wide heterogeneity in a secondary criterion of grouping will still develop discipline problems.

Just how great a distance can exist among group members in one criterion without disturbing the group balance is a problem that is still unsolved. Right now the situation has to be studied anew for each particular group. Research efforts to develop generally applicable standards are under way.

3. Practically any criterion may be relevant for grouping in one case and highly unimportant in another. The following, however, are generally the most important criteria in analyzing the causes of discipline problems:

Age and development—especially in physical and social maturity.

Socioeconomic, ethnic or racial backgrounds and the cultural differences brought about through sub-stratifications in our society. The differences in code between youngsters who are highly "manner-minded" and those who are proudly unconventional, for instance, or between those who admire or avoid fighting, should be considered more often.

Home acceptance or emancipation. Differences in dependency upon adults often count heavily during the upper elementary and the junior high school years, when children make the transition from highly home-identified to highly emancipation-greedy at varying rates.

Shyness-toughness. Some shy children together with a few more expressive ones make a good mixture. If the distance between them is too great, however, the shy youngster gets more scared than he was before and becomes a problem through his withdrawal. The wild one gets more show-offish through the easy admiration he gets from his more retiring colleagues.

Intelligence and knowledge—so well known that comment here is not needed.

Interest and work acceptance—especially vital in terms of learning morale.

Physical coordination—extreme differences in this characteristic tend to develop sharp sub-grouping within a group.

Leader acceptance—may range from open defiance to strong need for childlike dependence. These two tastes are hard for any teacher-leader to satisfy in one and the same group.

Organizational maturity—when two-thirds of your group could be expected to be self-governing while one-third of the youngsters are on such a level of organizational dependence that they cannot function without the pressure of outside lures and controls.

Enjoyment of group life—a factor which separates the happily group-eager youngster from his more isolationist pal.

All in all, the mere mixture in your group of too heterogeneous elements in criteria which are highly group-relevant may in itself be a constant producer of discipline problem behavior without anything else being wrong. Discovery and repair in time will save you much undeserved criticism and much self-accusation. A psychological analysis of your group composition therefore is a job well worth undertaking from time to time.

Know Your Groups

Needless to say, any one of the six group psychological factors in discipline problems may be coexistent with any other. Thus, the task for the practitioner boils down to this:

1. Do not allow yourself to be fooled by the surface appearance of a discipline problem. What youngsters do and how they act are not clear indications of the real source of your discipline problem.

2. You can find the trouble, though, by analyzing your discipline problems with these questions:

a. What does the behavior observed really mean?

b. To what extent is the behavior produced by the peculiar case history of the individual involved? To what extent does it also contain elements of a group psychological nature?

c. Which of the group psychological factors producing problem behavior are involved and to what degree?

3. On this basis you will want to add these further questions, growing out of a previous chapter, into your calculations:

a. Since I want to do something about it, what do I plan mainly for effect on the individual, what for effect on the group, and how can I respect the law of "marginal antisepsis"?

b. In which direction do I have to aim—the change of surface behavior or the modification of basic attitudes? How can I respect the law of marginal antisepsis with regard to this problem?

c. How can I evaluate whether what I want to do will "work" without being fooled by false analogies, or by the cheap sellers of "bags full of tricks" and without neglecting the less visible subsurface effects over the more visible and tangible result?

All this is not meant to substitute for the teacher's personal analysis of each case and of each situation. It is meant to encourage teachers to think through their own group problem instead of applying recommended techniques without critical examination.

Teachers are often troubled about their "consistency." Many seem to fear that it is somehow wrong to temper consequences for an individual child because of his anxieties and sensitivities. At other times teachers wonder if they are right to hold to penalties that have been agreed upon in advance. We cannot stress too often that consistency does not lie in a set repertory of standard penalties. Because individuals differ so widely in what they have experienced in the past and what they need in the future this is indeed the height of psychological inconsistency. Groups vary, too, in security and insight and are played upon by many dynamic influences. Consistency for the teacher-leader results through an analytic study of causes and through the clarity of purpose toward which action is directed in any given incident.

The authors are convinced that the good disciplinarian, while always retaining some of the qualities of an artist, is closer to the modern physician than to the performer of magical tricks at a county fair.

Discipline and Teacher Personality

Among the futile controversies which sometimes block progress at teachers conferences and in college courses is the well-known alternative of what makes you a good disciplinarian—your personality or your technical skill?

The frequency of this question and the dignified facial expressions of those who ask it, are likely to fool the practitioner on the job.

The truth is—the whole question is silly. There is no such alternative. The question is nothing but a magician's stunt invented to prolong discussion time and to conceal how little we really know about the issue. The facts behind the problem can simply be summarized in a few points:

1. "Personality" and "technical skill" are never in conflict with each other. Instead, they are complementary. One is meaningless without the other. There is no either-or situation involved.

2. Confusion is mainly nourished by a widespread abuse of the term "technical skill." Some people mean by "technical skill" the possession of a bag full of little "tricks" and "devices" which they think are "right" in themselves and the application of which they recommend to any discipline problem. If this abuse of the term, "technical skill," is referred to, then we would have to admit that teacher personality can do very well without it. Many teachers, who do not worry or even try to accumulate these little tricks, have the stuff it takes to meet children, and are doing very well.

However, the term "technical skill" may be given a deeper meaning which covers the following:

a. Knowledge of the human child and his developmental stages and of the laws of human behavior individually and in groups.

b. Ability to size up and analyze the situation as to its individual and group psychological involvements.

c. Knowledge of the techniques of human influence and their relationship to certain developmental ages and personality types.

d. The ability to figure out just which of these human influence techniques fits which situation and to make a fair estimate of the possible subsurface effects which need to be considered.

"Technical skill" as defined here, then, is highly essential, and not even the genius or the most perfect teacher personality could do without it.

3. What do we mean by "teacher personality," anyway? This is not the place to solve the entangled problem of what constitutes "best" teacher personality. The authors, however, do believe that the problem is not as "intangible" as it is often made out to be and that a list of about two dozen of the most vital traits for the successful and hygienic disciplinarian could be established.

One remark about teacher personality seems so essential here that we cannot postpone mentioning it. A sense of humor is obviously the most essential characteristic of skillful handlers of discipline problems or tough group situations and its possession must be among the prime requisites of the teacher. If we had to list also the one personality trait most injurious to successful discipline, we would mention for first choice: false dignity. No other single personality trait causes so much confusion, uproar and mismanagement. Unfortunately, we have to leave it to the imagination of the reader to figure out just how we do and how we do not mean this.

4. Where the ideal balance between "teacher personality" and "technical skill" should be is hard to state. It seems obvious, though, that certain jobs in this discipline business need a different emphasis than do certain others. These would be our hunches on the point:

For establishing good discipline and maintaining it (by discipline we mean here "order"), the personality of the teacher seems the most essential factor. Under ordinary circumstances, a teacher could get along well with few technical skills if this one factor is strongly represented.

For discovering sources of discipline problems and of doing a repair job in "discipline cases," even the most ideal personality equipment would not suffice. These jobs are closer to the work of the surgeon than to that of the artist, and special knowledge and technical skill weigh very heavily indeed.

5. One of the serious impediments in the development of disciplinary skills among teachers seems to be a peculiar misuse of "evaluation," particularly by people in supervisory positions. Evaluation of the disciplinary skills of teachers is more often off the beam than the evaluation of any other of their skills.

The most frequent mistakes in the evaluation of teachers' real disciplinary skills are these:

a. We confuse a teacher's skill in teaching and establishing order with her skill in handling incidents of conflict and disturbance. Often we load good practitioners in the first skill with the other task of counseling, to the disadvantage of all. Or, the other way around, we confuse psychological analysis of other people's discipline problems with the skill of establishing good organization in one's own group and end up with great surprises all around.

b. We blame a teacher for the individual problem child who may turn up in a group or praise a teacher for the lack of such problem cases. The teacher's own behavior is only one of the manifold factors going into the production of problem behavior in children and many of the others are entirely out of reach.

c. We praise or blame the teacher in terms of "success" in handling problem cases. Yet we know equally well that the teacher's own activity is only one among a wide variety of factors on which success or failure depends, and most of which are far beyond the teacher's reach.

d. We evaluate a teacher's handling of discipline by criteria which have nothing to do with teaching goals and conditions.

On the positive side we can say this about evaluation of disciplinary skills:

a. The occurrence or non-occurrence of discipline problems may not be under the control of the teacher at all. Why there is such occurrence or non-occurrence must be carefully studied before any evaluation is made.

Example: The teacher with a few especially disturbed children in a class must have more blow-ups happen than the teacher without such cases. The teacher in a school where community strife is vehement will not be able to avoid group conflict no matter how well discipline is planned.

b. Success or failure in meeting the disciplinary challenge may not be in the power of the teacher at all. Evaluations should not be made before this point is clearly determined.

Example: Everything Miss Jones did for Johnny was right. But his home situation was so mixed up that it was not possible for her to repair the youngster. At the same time Miss Smith worked with a youngster, made many mistakes, but parental cooperation was so excellent that the case turned into a complete "success."

c. Only criteria which are inherent in the situation we talk about should be used for an evaluation of skillful or wrong handling.

Example: Miss White built her discipline on the plan of developing attitude changes in her school-hostile clientele. Then her discipline should not be evaluated on the question of how well she subdued them.

d. Only the intellectual and emotional level on which a teacher approaches a discipline case can be used as criteria, for that is the portion which is at least partly within the teacher's power and reflects personal and professional growth.

Example: Miss Mills simply blew up at George's behavior, without thinking at all. This does not constitute wise disciplinary planning. Or, Miss Roberts had an elaborate plan for getting at the problem of the seventh grade. The plan was thoughtful and well founded. It did happen that her plan was opposed by the principal or by an incident which she could not have foreseen. Evaluation of her work should be based on the first, not the second, criterion.

e. Administratively, an open and clear policy of evaluation of teacher behavior along these lines would do a lot to help teachers *want* to become better disciplinarians. Too often they are told to do what is right by the principles of education in a democracy but are really evaluated according to surface effect, administrative tastes, community opposition, or superficial comfort in the administrative machinery. The real hinge is in the principal's office.

This last statement is perhaps the most hopeful of all. For it may be hard to reach all teachers in a country as vast as this. The number of principals in the United States is tremendous, too, but this group is of a size which can be contacted. The channels to reach the principals are well paved because of the nature of administrative jobs.

Before You Go Back to Your Classroom—Remember This

We do not believe the tremendous issue of "discipline" can be taught in a few sententious words. However, an occasional guidepost is often a help to the hurried practitioner on the job. We would, therefore, like to end this rather detailed discussion in a somewhat untraditional way, by suggesting the following thoughts for the teacher who is stepping into a classroom after reading all this:

1. **Routine tricks aren't the whole show. You can't sew discipline together out of rags.** Often, especially when we get jittery or when non-understanding superiors or colleagues put the thumbscrews upon us for the wrong things, we develop undue admiration for the organizational "gadget." We develop the illusion that the gadget could do the trick for us, would save us thinking, planning, loving, and understanding. Well, it won't. If you overload your group atmosphere with the rattle of organizational machinery—try to have a "rule" for everything under the sun and another principle of revenge, if that rule is broken, for everything under the moon—you are just going to thwart your best efforts in the long run. Don't think you have to run around with your belt stuck full of guns and lollipops all the time, either. Rely a little more on yourself, your "person," and your sense of humor. It saves you lots of headaches and leads to disciplinary poise.

2. The "mystery of personality" is good, when it works. But it is a poor excuse for failure. This second statement is to keep you from falling into the opposite extreme after reading the first. While our personality—and the way we get it across to children—establishes most of what we call "respect" and "leadership," there is also the "everyday trifle" that is more easily settled through a rule or common agreement than by your magic gaze. Children have, although sometimes they are unconscious of it, considerable need for regularity and predictability in what is expected. If their *whole* life is dependent on the whims of your genius, little frictions begin to increase. So, don't extend your contempt for using routine tricks instead of personality into mistaken contempt for *any* planning and organization.

3. Don't try to wash all your laundry with the same cake of soap. Sometimes we discover two or three nice little tricks that work. Then we develop the delusion that, if we just keep on sticking to these tricks, the rest of the problems of life will dissolve. Well, it won't wash. Don't expect tricks to work under all circumstances, and don't blame yourself or the children. Blame those tricks or, better, blame the way you translated them without enough planning.

Watch out, when you begin to tell "anecdotes" of how this or that "always works," for these are the moments when mental petrification begins.

4. Children are at least as complicated as a piece of wood. So you had better find out about their texture, elasticity and grain fiber before you apply your various tools and machinery upon them. Sometimes we want to get places fast, and then we spoil the whole show by using too coarse an instrument. If you do that, don't blame it on the instrument but upon your incomplete analysis of your material.

5. If you make a fool of yourself, why not be the first one to find out and have a good laugh about it? The worst superstition about discipline is that "respect" and "leadership" melt as easily as a chocolate bar. It is not true. If they do, they never were "real" respect and leadership to begin with.

So don't be jittery for fear that you will "jeopardize" your dignity in the eyes of your youngsters if they find out you aren't the Archangel Michael after all. The fear of exposure to ridicule has caused more intangible discipline problems than anything else. There is a difference between the laughter you start, and ridicule. Real, especially self-directed humor is the most disarming thing in the work with children that you could find.

6. **Don't develop suicidal fantasies, just because you aren't almighty after all.** There are limits to the power of the biggest magician among us as well as to the omnipotence of the most conscientious scientist. Every once in awhile we run up against those discoveries. If you do so, don't blame your youngsters because they can't be cured by you, nor blame yourself. The biggest hurdle in our work is time. It takes at least as many months of planful work to undo a wrong trait in a child as it took years of planful mishandling to build the wrong trait. But don't forget, many things can be started on the right track through long-range planning, though those same things can't be followed through to their final development. Don't be afraid of making mistakes. It isn't one particular mistake that produces distorted children—it is the wrong way of reacting to the mistakes after we make them. And that is entirely in your power.

7. **What do you want to be, anyway, an educator, or an "angel with the flaming sword"?** It is upon your answer to this question that your decisions about discipline techniques will finally depend. For it requires one type of person to be the proud avenger of infantile wrongs and sins against defied "rules and regulations," and another to be the guide of human beings through the turmoil of growth. You have to make up your mind.

8. **Remember you're human, too.** Many of the understandings required of you as a teacher today come into conflict with values learned before you can remember. In our earliest years, we accept certain behaviors of adults toward children and of children toward adults as "right" and natural. These convictions were learned in close emotional relationship with our own parents and teachers and are painful to change. It is hard to be objective about the child who still exists within each of us. Perhaps you have already realized that not all parents are like yours and that each child must be helped to grow wholesomely in his world as it is. Then you are well on your way to the emotional maturity, the sense of perspective and the freedom from threat needed by leaders of today's children and youth.

References

Association for Childhood Education International. *Discipline for Freedom.* Washington, D. C.: the Association, 1200 Fifteenth Street, N. W., 1951.

Association for Supervision and Curriculum Development. *Growing Up in An Anxious Age.* Washington, D. C.: the Association, a department of the NEA, 1952.

Association for Supervision and Curriculum Development. *Fostering Mental Health in Our Schools.* Washington, D. C.: the Association, a department of the NEA, 1950.

Baruch, Dorothy W. *Parents and Children Go to School.* New York: Scott Foresman and Co., 1939.

Buhler, C.; Smitter, F.; and Richardson, S. *Childhood Problems and the Teacher.* New York: Henry Holt and Co., Inc., 1952.

Buxbaum, Edith. *Your Child Makes Sense.* New York: International Universities Press, Inc., 1949.

Coladarci, Arthur P. "The Class as a Group." *Educational Psychology* (A book of readings). New York: Dryden Press, 1955. Chapter IV.

Cunningham, Ruth, et al. *Understanding Group Behavior of Boys and Girls.* New York: Bureau of Publications, Teachers College, Columbia University, 1950.

Hymes, James L., Jr. *A Pound of Prevention.* New York: Caroline Zachry Institute of Human Development, New York State Commission on Mental Hygiene, 1947.

Hymes, James L., Jr. *Behavior and Misbehavior.* New York: Henry Holt and Co., Inc., 1955.

Lewin, Kurt. *Resolving Social Conflicts.* New York: Harper and Bros., 1948.

National Education Association, Research Division. "Teacher Opinion on Pupil Behavior, 1955-56." *Research Bulletin* 34: 51-107; April 1956.

Redl, Fritz, and Wattenberg, W. *Mental Hygiene in Teaching.* New York: Harcourt Brace & Co., 1951.

Redl, Fritz, and Wineman, David. *Children Who Hate.* Glencoe, Illinois: The Free Press, 1951.

Redl, Fritz, and Wineman, David. *Controls From Within.* Glencoe, Illinois: The Free Press, 1952.

Slavson, S. R. *Creative Group Education.* New York: Association Press, 1940, p. 247.

Wattenberg, William. *The Adolescent Years.* New York: Harcourt Brace & Co., 1955.

51871